GUIDED MEDITATION FOR ANXIETY

Your New Path to Avoid Fidgety State, Achieve Stress Relief and Eliminate Any Sign of Anger, Depression and Panic Attack, Using Mindfulness Techniques in Plain English

Table of Contents

Chapter 4. The Best Kind of Meditation Done for You

Chapter 5. How to Set Your Mind to Make Meditation a Habit

Introduction

What is Mindfulness?

First, a bit of history. Mindfulness is a form of meditation that primarily comes out of the Buddhist Theravada tradition, though elements of it are also found in Zen Buddhism and some in Tibetan Buddhism. Western Buddhist Vipassana meditation evolved from the Buddhist Theravada tradition, and the mindfulness movement comes from that.

In Buddhist meditation, there are three yanas, or vehicles. This refers to modes of spiritual practice and schools of Buddhism. These include Hinayana, the basic or foundational vehicle; Mahayana, the second or great vehicle; and Vajrayana, the third, also known as the diamond or tantric vehicle. As one goes through the vehicles, the later ones build on and incorporate the elements of each other. The stages of spiritual development in the Hinayana are calm abiding, or Shamatha, and clear seeing, or Vipashyana, which includes non-self. In the Mahayana vehicle, one adds bodhicitta, and emptiness of things, or Shunyata. In Vajrayana, one desires to train this mind of ours and develop pure perception, to experience the true nature of mind and clear light.

Mindfulness meditation is associated with the first yana, or vehicle, and mindfulness is unique in that it takes and incorporates the techniques of Buddhist attention and mind training but strips away the religious trappings, beliefs, ceremony, and vows. It is not affiliated with any religion. By studying mindfulness meditation, you gain the tools, skills, and benefits of mind training without any of the religious obligations.

Admittedly, some of this may sound quite foreign and abstract, but the actual process of mindfulness is usually very simple. Mindfulness is simply paying attention, noticing without judgment, and being present in whatever you're doing. As most people go about their daily lives, their minds wander to other thoughts or sensations, instead of being present with the actual activities they are participating in. Through mindfulness practice, we learn to be actively and more fully involved in these activities instead of allowing our minds to wander.

Why Mindfulness Works

Mindfulness meditation provides you with the ability to train your mind to focus and maintain your attention, to remain in the present moment or nowness, and to approach life events and whatever arises in your mind or in the world with an open, non-judgmental, and caring attitude. The more we are aware of the present moment, firmly grounded in it, and acting from it, the better life is in all regards. Whatever we are doing, we become better at it.

What is Meditation?

There are a number of possible definitions of meditation, and we will look at several of them. Meditation is an activity, usually connected with spirituality and found in all of the great religions, designed to transform the mind and heart and sometimes the body, and the goal is to move towards and through the stages of self-realization or enlightenment. There are many different forms of meditation, including concentration, openness, analysis, insight, awareness, clarity, calmness, self-love, compassion, visualization, chanting, and movement.

Meditation is a process through which we get to know how our mind works and train our attention to remain where we place it. My teacher used to say that his mind and attention were as "steady and stable as a cup sitting on a table!" By practicing meditation, we can get used to remaining present, undisturbed by whatever thoughts, emotions, or sensations arise. Our mind remains focused and steady. In its most simple form, meditation is just focusing our attention on something, in the here and now, and maintaining our attention, largely undistracted.

Meditation is about learning to simply be present with whatever arises in our mind and awareness. As things arise, we find ourselves able to remain more neutral and not identify with or grasp onto them. This is especially helpful in the arising of troubling thoughts, upsetting emotions, and unsettling sensations.

In meditation, there are things to gain and things to eliminate, and these usually happen simultaneously. For example, we need to develop our focus and concentration and eliminate our distractions and discursive thinking. As some develop, others naturally fall away. We need to gain compassion, love, and acceptance (for ourselves and others) and to let go of loathing, judgment, criticism, anger, and hate (for ourselves and others).

In meditation, we have the opportunity to examine our thoughts and emotions, our motivations, our actions and reactions, and the way in which we see the world. We actually get to discover who we really are.

Why Meditation Works

All great religions, and most likely all cultures, have their own forms of meditation, and different types of meditation have been in existence for literally thousands of years. Mindfulness meditation, derived from Buddhism, has been in existence for about 2,600 years. Hindu and Taoist meditations have some similarities and have been around for approximately 4,000 and 2,000 years, respectively. While Tibetan Buddhism has not been in existence for that long, it was so integrated into their entire culture and daily life that everything revolved around it, thus speeding its development. Also, the "best and brightest" in the Tibetan culture were selected to study and develop the areas of meditation and spirituality. Instead of their high achievers becoming doctors, lawyers, CEOs, or politicians, they became spiritual scholars and meditation masters, strongly elevating and developing the field of meditation. Mindfulness meditation is simple, straightforward, well researched, and imminently practical.

Mindfulness For Anxiety: A New Model For Treatment

Regularly engaging in mindfulness meditation has been shown to significantly reduce anxiety, as well as stress and other negative or difficult emotions. However, the combination of therapies and mindfulness meditation you will learn in this book is something entirely new—it has not been presented before. It comes out of the culmination of my four decades of education, training, experience, and the synthesis of numerous fields of study and methods of psychotherapy. I've used it myself and with hundreds of clients over many years and get frequent reports as to its effectiveness.

As I mentioned earlier, mindfulness and meditation can occur anytime we focus our attention, largely undistracted. For example, you can focus on your breath, emotion, sensation, movement, the sky, nature, a picture, a candle, and so on. What we're doing here is using various methods to work with anxiety.

Let's take a look at the theory first. In traditional psychotherapy, we often focus on the story of the circumstances, and the thoughts we are having about the circumstances. For example, perhaps someone is dealing with a divorce and the idea of how they will cope with the financial or emotional burden of living alone. Some therapies then add in awareness of the emotions and suggestions on how to manage them. This might include awareness of anxiety or stress and then therapy and meditation suggested as management tools. In the somatic, or body-based, approaches to psychology, one may encounter and focus on various physical experiences. The individual might explore why their hands shake or their heart pounds when they enter the courtroom or see their spouse. However, these physical experiences are often not well integrated with the other two approaches that focus on thoughts and emotions because we don't usually think of sensations as having much importance in psychotherapy and healing. This approach is still relatively new.

I suggest that we consider that psychological issues exist simultaneously on all three levels. The mind, located in the head, is the center of thoughts and cognition. The heart is the center of emotions and love and is located in the center of the chest, while the body is the center of energy and power and is primarily located in the lower abdomen (though it includes the entire body). The mind center corresponds to thinking and telling the story about things. The heart center corresponds to various troubling emotions as well as love and compassion. The body center corresponds to energy and power and also includes any physical experiences throughout the body.

The major problem is that we tend to live our life in our head, in our thoughts and stories, cut off from our actual experience. Just like when we go out to eat, the menu is not the food, and when we're out and about, the map is not the actual territory, the thoughts about our experience is not the experience itself. We get lost in our mental ruminations and incessant worrying, and we miss the actual experience. We must put aside the digressive thinking and be mindful and aware of our actual emotional and physical experiences as they occur. This shift is the basis for what comes next: how to directly work with these experiences and transform them.

What actually shifts, lessens, and dissolves troubling emotions and physical experiences is the mindful awareness of them in the moment. Please reread that statement and think about it, as this is so very important. This is the basis for how meditation works in many of the great religions of the world: just being aware of our thoughts, emotions, and physical experiences with a focused but spacious awareness allows them to transform. This may take the form of changing, dissolving, lessening, or gaining insight about them. I remember the moment that I discovered this, and it was a life-altering moment for me. This fundamental approach has been providing psychological help and relief for people for thousands of years.

There are some old adages that point to this such as: "Be with what is, moment by moment," and "What you can be with, will let you be, and what you can't be with, won't let you be." Let's explore what the term "be with" is referring to, as this is both the crux of the matter and the heart of mindfulness meditation. We get lost in our mind's ruminative thinking, going around and around and stirring our anxiety higher and higher. We only make things worse. We believe that if we can only understand the problem, then it will be solved. This is especially prevalent in our very mentalistic, cognitively oriented, and generally well-educated culture. Unfortunately, it is just not true. The way out of this conundrum is to simply be aware, moment by moment, of our actual emotional and physical experiences, as well as aware of our thoughts. This awareness of the experiences combined with the act of staying with them allows troubling experiences and problems to shift and dissolve. It is both my belief and experience that this is exactly how it works.

I further suggest that we should use this fundamental approach in combination with some of the most effective practices of modern psychology.

Combining Therapies

In psychology, a few therapies are recognized to be particularly effective. These include such modalities as cognitive behavioral therapy (CBT), EMDR (eye movement desensitization reprocessing), and the use of mindfulness. In addition to these, I use somatic focusing, which is the noticing of physical locations and sensations, as well as directing the breath into, through, or around these areas and sensations. My specific approach to breathing is derived from decades of studying breathwork, a Westernized form of breathing, similar to Kundalini yoga, but non-religious and significantly modified to provide a gentle and very safe approach to working with issues. The combination of these modalities has proven to be very effective and teachable. I get regular reports from clients as to how they use this approach, the various issues and situations they utilize it with, and the consistent results they achieve.

One other important thing that I do is add spaciousness to the mindfulness meditation. Typically, a mindfulness meditation is more of a concentrative meditation, where we mostly emphasize the ability to focus the mind, and as such, it has more involvement with thoughts. The main type of meditation that I do, Buddhist Dzogchen meditation, emphasizes awareness, spaciousness, and resting in that. When this type of approach is used on anxiety, the effects are multiplied exponentially. Many clients are able to focus their minds on their experiences, gently breathe into and through the sensations, allow the emotions to simply be there, and rest in the open space with it. It's a very calming and peaceful practice as well as an incredibly effective one.

Finally, I include many other types of therapy in conjunction with the therapy I just described as the fundamental skill or approach. As things begin to change to a more open and relaxed feeling, I find it is a really good time to include CBT therapy. Otherwise, it is like trying to teach someone to swim when they are deathly afraid of the water. One must get rid of some of the excessive negative emotion for the cognitive piece to really be effective. Eventually, most clients gain some expertise in finding a more mentally and emotionally open place while being with their experiences, and then they can reason with themselves in healthy and appropriate ways.

How Mindfulness Meditations Ease Anxiety

Research on meditation in general began in the late 1960s with the Transcendental Meditation movement and has steadily progressed from there. Today, a considerable amount of scientific research exists regarding why and how meditation works, much of which has come out over the last three decades and especially the last ten years.

When we look at neuroscience in particular, scientists have been studying the physical effects of meditation for about 20 years using MRIs and other techniques. Research on neuroplasticity indicates that the human brain does not go into decline after a few decades of life, as was originally thought, but can change and evolve throughout adulthood and even into old age. We can form new connections and neurons, while learning new skills and engaging in mental challenges, throughout our life span.

Interesting research results reveal what happens inside the brain and how the brain changes with meditation. Mindfulness meditation appears to activate and increase the density of certain areas, while decreasing the activity and size of others. Some of the main areas that are activated and increase in density include the following:

- INSULA: associated with compassion, self-awareness, and empathy
- LEFT HIPPOCAMPUS: essential for memory. Helps us learn by increasing cognitive ability and recall, as well as

increasing self-awareness, empathy, and emotional regulation.

- PUTAMEN: involved in learning

- INTERIOR CINGULATE CORTEX: regulates heart rate, blood pressure, breathing, and other autonomic functions

- POSTERIOR CINGULATE: associated with discursive thoughts and self-relevance (the amount of subjectivity and self-referral when processing information). The larger and stronger the posterior cingulate is, the fewer wandering and discursive thoughts we will have and the more realistic our sense of self will be. This area increases our ability to stay aware of the present moment, without judgment, and to observe such things as sensations and emotions that rise in the moment without overly identifying with them.

- PREFRONTAL CORTEX: mediates more complex thinking skills such as planning, decision-making, and self-regulating our social behavior

- PONS: where many of the neurotransmitters are produced. Regulates essential functions including facial expressions, sleep, basic physical functioning, and processing sensory input.

- TEMPOROPARIETAL JUNCTION (TPJ): associated with empathy and compassion, being humane and just, as well as our sense of perspective. This area becomes more active when we place ourselves in someone else's shoes, thus seeing and feeling things from their perspective.

I saved one of the most important areas for last: the amygdala. The previously mentioned brain areas all increase in activity, as well as size and gray matter density, but the amygdala is the one area of the brain that, when it changes through meditation, actually shrinks. This area of the brain produces feelings of anxiety, fear, reactivity, and general stress—and it is physically smaller in the brains of expert meditators.

Even just eight weeks of regular meditation can lead to a measurable decrease in the size of the amygdala. A smaller amygdala is associated with fewer strong emotional responses such as anxiety and "fight or flight." Changes in the brain caused by even a relatively small amount of meditation can leave us feeling significantly calmer and less anxious, with an increased sense of well-being.

On a whole-body level, some common effects of meditation include reduced pulse, lowered and more stable blood pressure, better sleep and reduced insomnia, increased cognition and recall, and reduced levels of cortisol, a hormone related to stress and adrenal fatigue. There are also numerous reports that show meditation reducing the amount of pain medication needed. One recent study showed that taking a break to practice mindfulness meditation was even better than a walk in nature for relaxing, refreshing, and revitalizing oneself.

Here is a final, short anecdotal story regarding my own experience with the effects of meditation. A couple of years ago, I was lying on a gurney in the procedure room awaiting a routine colonoscopy. I was connected to vitals monitoring and was being quizzed by the anesthesiologist to determine the amount of sedative Propofol to give me. He suddenly asked me if I had taken any anti-anxiety or other mood-altering medications prior to my arrival. I told him that I had not, and I expected him to move on with the questioning. However, he persisted, assuring me that it was "really okay if I had, but I just need to know," so that he could factor that into the anesthesia dose. Again, I assured him that I had not, at which time he paused and explained that my blood pressure was only 103/62 and pulse was 61, and that in all of his years of medical practice he had never had somebody with such low vital stats when they were about to undergo such a procedure. With a puzzled look, he glanced down and queried, "Okay, so what's your secret?" I looked up at him, smiled gently, and replied, "I meditate." He looked back at me with a big grin, shook his head, and exclaimed, "Wow, nice!"

Chapter 1. Recognize Your Emotion

Your feelings are critical to your ability to acclimate to the troubles of your step by step life. When you feel much improved, you're prepared to negligence even the most abusive of tasks, yet when you're miserable, you view even a lovely development with a sentiment of sadness and destiny. Feelings in like manner impact our relationship with others. If a sidekick uncovers to you a grievous story and you react by giggling instead of looking appalling or concerned, you'll give off an impression of being rude and uncaring. On the other hand, in case you glower when you should smile at your sidekick's jokes, you'll cause offense for different reasons.

Becoming violently unhinged to a minor irritation can cause you to appear hyper or even lopsided. Then again, in the event that you respond with undue satisfaction to a respectably minor piece of inspiring news, people will in like manner examine your improvement and adequacy. Newborn children are allowed to shout with joy or cry with fierceness yet as adults; we're depended upon to deal with the outward showing of our feelings.

If you need all the more inducing about the activity of feelings in our ability to succeed or tumble in standing up to life's challenges, consider a part of the outstanding people whose callings have been fixed by the less than ideal show of their feelings. In the fundamental keep running up to the 2004 presidential choice, Howard Senior member's office finished for all intents and purposes medium-term after his "YAAAAHHH" minute turned into a medium-term Web sensation. Edmund Muskie, in the 1972 fundamental season, presented a similar political socially awkward act in which he shed tears consequent to winning the New Hampshire basic (anyway he ensured they were snowflakes sparkling close to the start of the sunshine). Out of the blue, tears are very prominent in the post-2000 political world. Hillary Clinton wasn't seen as astute enough until her eyes blurred over while tending to a voter's request (again in New Hampshire!), yet numerous intellectuals utilized this against her to scrutinize her earnestness. At that point, there's the nostalgic carryings-on of House Republican pioneer John Boehner, whose tear channels appear on steady overdrive.

These models show not just that the outward showcase of internal sentiments impacts how we're respected by others, yet in addition that these passionate presentations are vigorously subject to social standards. To be viewed as a well-adjusted individual from the society we have to cling to those standards or hazard judgment or scorn. Specialist Paul Ekman exhibited that there are six fundamental feelings that people of all social orders involvement and see (bliss, inconvenience, stun, shock, fear, and sicken). How and when we express these feelings fluctuates in a general sense by the guidelines of all of our social orders, the alleged grandstand rules.

Our emotions sway the way wherein others treat us, in any case, our inward assumption of prospering. We will decide in doubt recognize that whether we are encountering positive or negative emotions reflects controls past our ability to deal with, accusing everything from our attributes to the climate. In any case, what different individuals don't grasp is that sentiments aren't carefully obliged by your body's physiology the way that reflexes are. You're not stuck for life with the energized apparatus modified into your DNA.

To comprehend the way where that you can control your emotions, from the outset we need to take a slight bypass through the early history of mind science.

Perspectives about what emotions are, and what causes them, have changed altogether in the last 100 or so years. To take this experience, who loved in any case eventually William James, the organizers of American cerebrum ask about?

As shown by James, and the undauntedly related perspectives on physiologist Carl Lange, your sentiments are totally addressed by your body's reactions. In all honesty, they are the sentiments. Envision you're being searched for after by a bear. In the occasion that you're similar to the greater part of us, dread and free for all will acknowledge order over your whole nearness, making your heart race, your palms to get sweat-sprinkled, and your stomach to turn somersaults. James and Lange broke down these reactions of your autonomic unmistakable structure with the credible feeling of dread. As indicated by their hypothesis, your significant response doesn't look for after the tendency, it is the tendency. As James communicated, "Sound judgment says we lose our fortune, are deplored and cry; we meet a bear, are surprised and run; we are irritated by an opponent, are rankled and strike, dreadful in light of the manner in which that we tremble... the more customary assertion is that we feel sorry in light of the way that we cry, irate in light of the way that we strike, uneasy in light of the way that we tremble." As a matter of fact, when a "characteristic" (or gut) vigorous response came around they would not joke about this.

Various people found the James-Lange speculation hard to recognize. Sound judgment seems to work out okay, despite James' assertion. Beside the theory essentially "feeling" mistakenly (so to speak), it in like manner fail to meet the preliminary of coherent value and was along these lines over the long haul dropped as an explanation.

The thalamus may be locked in with some exciting rule, anyway it's not the cerebrum's concern zone for our conclusions. Or maybe, the amygdala is apparently the guilty party concerning such feelings as fear, savagery, and jealousy.

The possibility that our emotions might be controllably begun to rise in the hypothesis created by Stanley Schachter and Jerome Singer in the mid-1960s. In their now exemplary brain research explore, they drove understudies to accept that they were getting a preliminary portion of a nutrient. Truth be told, the experimenters infused the understudies with epinephrine. The understudies at that point watched a "confederate" (another understudy carrying on test guidelines) who turned out to be either irate or euphoric while finishing a lot of polls. The understudies presented to the irate confederate announced that they felt furious; those presented to the euphoric confederate said they felt cheerful. The outcomes demonstrated that the blend of energy (realized by epinephrine) and setting (the confederate's direct) influenced the eager state of the exploratory subject.

To disentangle, the Schachter-Vocalist study surmises that your feelings are influenced by what's going on in the people around you and which feelings they're conveying. Another articulation for this is "energetic malady." On the off chance that you've any time felt moved to cry at the wedding of people you don't know very well since everyone around you is crying into their hankies, you know how these assessments can jump on.

Your feelings don't have to fall prey to those being impacted by the people around you, be that as it may. The mental uprising in inclination theory, driven by College of Pennsylvania specialist Aaron Beck, showed that our thoughts alone can make our feelings. Beck's examinations of debilitated individuals drove him to the revelation that wrecked airs and contrarily encircled programmed considerations are at the base of individuals' sentiments of misery. A pointless outlook is a strategy for study the world that spotlights on the negative and strange pieces of your experiences. An unfavorably encompassed customized thought is an unaware conviction that spotlights on your deficiencies instead of your characteristics. Together, pointless mindsets and modified thoughts make the "negative gathering of three" including a negative viewpoint on yourself, your existence, and your future. The wide research subject to Beck's speculation has provoked affirmation of his mental social procedure for treatment as the head treatment of wretchedness.

Despite whether you're not clinically disheartened, you can get a page from Beck's playbook to grasp your feelings. For instance, sharpness is realized by the conviction that you've lost or will lose something basic to you, shock is brought about by the conviction that someone has expelled something from you, and uneasiness relies upon the conviction that something horrendous will come to pass. Strangely distorting your experiences conveys these contemplations which by then lead to your negative feelings. I ought to stop thinking this way. I see that I'm having nervous insights right now. What's an inexorably acceptable thought? What may I tell my dearest friend?

I should have the alternative to bounce on a plane without anxiety. I wish I wasn't so alarmed of flying, yet I recognize that I'm working at an answer. What might I have the option to do right now? Figuring out how to identify with others is a key ability in social collaborations. On the off chance that you comprehend what other individuals are thinking and feeling you'll have the option to be a superior companion and have better collaborations.

Be that as it may, to figure out how to feel for other people, you first need to figure out how to sympathize with yourself.

That sounds extremely delicate inclination yet stick with me. This is significant and fantastically viable. Figuring out how to sympathize with yourself means figuring out how to comprehend and acknowledge what you're feeling and for what reason you're feeling it.

In case you're feeling furious, you ought to have the option to remember "I feel irate" and comprehend the reasons why you feel irate. You ought to approve of inclination your emotions, and not overlook them or smother them.

In a general sense, if something downright terrible transpired; it ought to be OK that you feel dismal. You should give yourself the authorization to feel tragic. At times, we get this thought we have to act upbeat constantly, or that our issues are not as significant as the issues of others, so we feel egotistical when we are dismal or disturbed.

In any case, that is not valid. Your issues matter, since you matter. What's more, if something is going on to hurt you or make you feel tragic, it's alright to express that bitterness and to give yourself a chance to feel that pity. You don't need to keep that contained.

Tolerating Your Emotions

Obviously, it's a good thought to attempt to improve your circumstance so whatever is making you feel miserable isn't causing that bitterness any longer. You don't need to STAY miserable.

What's more, in spite of the fact that everybody gets pitiful or furious some of the time, on the off chance that it appears as though you're dismal or irate constantly the time, you should think earnestly about observing a guide. Much the same as a specialist can enable you to mend physically, an advocate can enable you to recuperate inwardly, and there's no disgrace in conversing with one.

That goes for something other than getting emotional, coincidentally. In case you're battling with misery or tension or dejection or any number of different things, see an advocate. There's no disgrace in it, and it may very well change - or spare - your life. (In the event that you have to converse with somebody immediately, call 1-800-442-HOPE and you'll be associated with a volunteer guide for nothing.)

However, the fact is that you should give yourself consent to encountering the sentiments you have. In the event that something terrible transpired, it's alright that you feel tragic. You should feel good telling loved ones what you're feeling, notwithstanding when you're not feeling positive, or notwithstanding when you don't know why you feel the manner in which you do. On a principal level, you ought to acknowledge that your emotions are a piece of you, and similarly, as you have to acknowledge yourself, you have to acknowledge your emotions.

Take a second and re-read through that passage once more. No, truly. Return and read it. I'll pause.

Understanding Your Emotions

Inquire as to whether these things are valid for you. Do you comprehend the reason for your emotions when you feel something? Do you give yourself consent to feel a feeling? Do you acknowledge that it's alright to feel the manner in which you do? Do you have a sound method to express those emotions?

On the off chance that the response to any of those inquiries is "No" or "I don't know," at that point set aside some effort to thoroughly consider how you experience emotions. Wonder why you are replying in that manner, and what you have to improve relations to yourself. Converse with somebody you trust and get their recommendation and backing, or think about making a meeting with an advocate.

It may require some investment to process through this, yet it merits the speculation. Having a strong and solid comprehension of your own emotions encourages you to carry on with a cheerful, sound life. People are passionate creatures, and your emotions are a piece of your identity.

Furthermore, obviously, emotions are a piece of every other person, as well. In the event that you comprehend what it resembles when you feel a feeling, you'll be better ready to comprehend and interface with an individual who is feeling something comparative. So regardless of whether you would prefer not to comprehend your emotions for the good of your own, do it for your associations with others. It's justified, despite all the trouble.

Thoroughly Considering It

I have an activity for you to do today. It may appear somewhat bizarre, however, trust me - I think you'll discover a lot of advantages to it.

As you experience the day, watch out for your emotions, and search for the occasions in which you are feeling something (regardless of whether that something is dissatisfaction or satisfaction or pity or fatigue or whatever else). At that point, set aside the effort to thoroughly consider for what reason you're feeling that way.

Thoroughly consider your feeling in the manner works best for you. Maybe you may put aside some time toward the day's end to take a walk, so you have a calm time to think. Maybe you could record your contemplations on your emotions for the afternoon and after that contrast your notes from various days with searching for patterns. Or on the other hand, maybe you ought to ask a companion or relative to enable you to comprehend your emotions and talk it over with them.

Whatever the outcome, I think you'll discover by the day's end you comprehend yourself somewhat better, which will make it simpler for you to get others. What's more, when you believe you are beginning to comprehend your own emotions, read on to discover how to comprehend the emotions of others.

Mastering your emotions is accomplished when you decide you do not want to be controlled by the negativity you confront in your life. This requires dedication and commitment but can be highly rewarding. When you learn to master your emotions, you are less likely to play the role of victim. Instead, you allow your emotions — the negative and the positive — to empower you. By developing your emotional intelligence skills, you have already laid the foundation to have complete control over your emotions. This can have a powerful impact on your success, relationships, health, and overall quality of life.

What makes mastering your emotions difficult is that we often automatically fall into negative thought patterns. Negative thoughts not only impact your emotional experience — they can completely dictate how you behave and react to emotional experiences, as well as determine which emotional experience you will have more of. By first understanding how these negative thought patterns affect your emotional health, you will be able to more clearly and intentionally shift your negativity to positive experiences and lessons.

Understanding negativity bias

Negativity bias is our unintentional focus on all the negative occurrences we face throughout the day. This is best understood when you are stuck in traffic and running late for work. Often, you tend to let this simple event dictate the rest of your day. Your attitude is often more negative, your behavior more hostile, and your emotions more out of control. Negativity bias simply means you spend too much time going over negative events, to the point that you miss out and fail to recognize the more positive experiences you could be having.

In order to gain more control over your emotions, have a more positive experience, and become more resilient through life's challenges, you must first address this simple issue of constantly focusing on the negative. When you only see and acknowledge the negative, it is easy to understand why you might only have negative experiences.

How to change your emotional state from stressed and negative to positive and productive

As you can see, negative thoughts tend to be our default. They are often deeply rooted in our behaviors and outlook on life. One of the first things to do to adopt a more positive and productive state is to begin wiring your brain to search for the positives in each day. When you catch yourself having negative thoughts, opinions, or emotions, counter this with at least three positive emotional experiences. Up until now, you have wired your brain to seek out the negative — this is why it seems so easy to get caught up in the negativity. But by shifting the ratio of negative and positive experiences so that you have more enjoyable moments, it will become second nature and more natural to find these positive parts of your day.

Once you have gotten a better handle on actively searching for positive experiences, there are more steps you can take to shift your stressed out and negative emotional experience to ones that will serve you in a more productive and positive way.

Learn to express your emotions

It is one thing to understand your emotions, but it is another thing to admit to the emotions you are experiencing. Often, we secretly deal with our emotions in private, because there tends to be a negative connotation associated with extreme negative emotions. For this reason, your emotions still have control over you. When you allow your emotions to force you to hide, deny, or cover up what you are feeling, you are not fully addressing them.

When you learn to properly express your emotions, you learn how to take control of them — and to control them in a way that moves you in a more positive direction. In order to express your emotions properly, you need to first be able to identify what you are feeling in the present moment. Practice properly expressing the emotion you are experiencing by stating these emotions out loud. When you announce these emotions, do so with confidence and empowerment. Stating your emotions to yourself out loud when you are alone will help you build confidence so you can properly state them out loud in front of others. When you feel comfortable enough, practice stating your emotions out loud to people you trust and feel safe with. You can begin this practice by focusing just on expressing your more positive emotions, and then begin to express your emotions when you are in more challenging situations. Remember that when you openly state your emotions, you are inviting others to do the same, and they may not feel the same way you do. Keep an open mind and remain confident about what you are feeling — don't let what others say sway you from your own experiences.

Tracking your emotions

One of the best ways to begin identifying how you handle stressful and negative situations is to keep track of them. Starting an emotional, or mood journal can help you better organize, understand, and change your negative thought patterns, behaviors, and emotional responses. Begin keeping a daily log of everything you experience throughout your day. How did you feel in each significant moment, and what were your thoughts as you were going through the motions?

When you do this daily over a long period of time, you will begin to take notice of some of your emotional patterns. You can clearly identify triggers that cause you to feel more negatively. This also allows you to pinpoint the thoughts that occur as you have emotional experiences. This simple exercise, which can be done in five or ten minutes, can help you strengthen your self-awareness.

Not only will journaling about your emotions allow you to change your negative experiences into positive ones, but the process can also be beneficial for your mental health. Getting these things out of your head can help reduce your risk of suffering from depression and anxiety. This is because you are not just keeping the experience stuck in your head and dwelling on one aspect of the event, which tends to be just the negative. When you write it down, you can clearly see what caused you to have such a negative reaction. This can then allow you to find a better way of dealing with situations like these in the future.

Take care of yourself

How you treat yourself can have a major impact on how you handle negative situations. As you learned earlier, the way you treat yourself impacts your confidence, and when you lack confidence, it will be more difficult to overcome your negative thought patterns. When you treat yourself with kindness and compassion, you're able to better confront negative situations and stress in a more calm and proactive way. In order to shift from constantly thinking things are stressful and negative, you want to be able to treat yourself in a way that allows you to make mistakes, take risks, and find solutions.

This is especially important when it comes to how you talk to yourself. If you find that your internal dialogue is one that constantly berates you, points out your failures, or keeps you feeling stuck and incapable, you need to first focus on shifting this negative mindset. A negative thought process will never allow you to see the positive in any situation, whether it is a joyful or unpleasant one.

Reframe your perspective

There are a number of ways to shift your perspective to better cope and to find the positive in most negative situations. You can begin by taking on a more positive outlook. Instead of being discouraged, hurt, or angry by a specific experience, learn to identify how the situation has healed you and allowed you to grow. You can also shift your perspective by looking at where you will be years from now. Many bad experiences are stressful and negative at the moment. Recall an event that you thought was the worst thing that could ever happen to you. Do you still have those same negative emotions? Chances are, you can probably look back and laugh at yourself for ever thinking that way. Before you begin to think about how bad a situation is, remember to look ahead and consider how you will view this situation in the future. Additionally, you can begin to understand your own worst-case perspective. This allows you to truly see the situation is not as bad as you are making it seem. To better utilize this shifting perspective, you want to identify the positive around each negative situation. You will begin to realize that there are plenty of things to be motivated and feel good about, despite things not turning out exactly how you had hoped.

You can also try taking an empathetic perspective to shift your attitude to a more positive and productive one. This type of perspective shifting provides you with the opportunity to see things from someone else's point of view. Many times, we can be so caught up in our own experience that we fail to recognize the other people around us and how they may be interpreting the same situation differently. When you take the time to look at things from another person's point of view, you can gain an understanding of how to let go of your own hurt feelings, resentment, and negative emotions to truly embrace the positives that are present.

Practice forgiveness

Forgiveness can provide you with a number of benefits, especially when it comes to accepting negative events. When you forgive yourself and others for any negativity, you will reduce your emotions of hurt, anger, and disappointment. Forgiveness is simply the act of acknowledging what occurred and letting it go so it does not have a greater negative effect on you.

Regaining positive emotions

It can seem impossible to experience positive emotions to the fullest extent when you have spent so much time allowing the negative ones to control your life. When this occurs, your brain is programmed to seek out more negative experiences, as this is what it is currently wired to do. When you want to attract more positive experiences your way, you need to first focus on retraining your brain to find them.

It can be easy to become overwhelmed by negative emotions, and these can quickly spiral into a state of mind that leaves you feeling lost and out of control. When you begin to notice you are feeling stuck, chronically stressed, and indecisive, there are simple steps that can help you have more positive experiences.

Ask yourself a lot of questions

Question what you are feeling, why you are feeling that way, what has occurred in your past that could be triggering your emotional response, and if the way you are behaving in reaction to these emotions causes you to look at these emotions in an adaptive or maladaptive way? Analyzing your emotions, the situation, and your behavior is one of the first ways you can begin to experience more positive emotions. Once you have answered these questions, you can use your answers to help you visualize better solutions. When you want to change your negative emotions to more positive ones, visualizing can allow you to clearly develop a specific solution for dealing with emotions.

Get involved in more healthy activities

Keeping your body healthy affects your emotional health, just as your emotional health affects your physical health. When you take the time to take care of yourself, you feel better about yourself, which results in more positive emotions. Find activities that make you feel good — this can include starting a new hobby, listening to music, being creative, and practicing physical activity.

Often, these types of activities can be combined, such as exercising while listening to uplifting music or finding a hobby that also allows you to be creative like painting, photography, or learning to play an instrument. Pushing yourself to try new things helps build your confidence, and when you have more confidence, you feel more in control and able to handle difficult situations.

Socialize and be available for others

When you know there is a situation, event, or encounter coming up that you recognize as something that will leave you feeling negative, talking with others can help in a number of ways. Reaching out to your support group can give you a new perspective on the upcoming situation, as well as provide you with positive feedback about how to handle it. Being social can also help reduce the stress and anxiety you may be feeling about the situation, because your support group can help you look at things realistically.

Aside from turning to your support system, when you make yourself more available to others, you can learn to strengthen your empathy. Opening up yourself to be supportive to others who are going through difficult times can bring you more awareness of how others respond to difficult situations and this, in return, can help you gain a better awareness of your own responses.

Emotions can be triggered by all sorts of things from people, places, and times of day or even certain objects. How triggers work is that they activate thoughts or memories in our brain and cause us to have physical and emotional responses.

Having emotions is a normal human reaction to our life circumstances, the problem comes when we are unable to evaluate our emotions or consider their impact on our lives. Most people passively accept their emotions; they don't even get to the points we have covered where they choose to identify what the emotion is or what has triggered it.

How Our Thoughts Shape Our Emotions

During the 1960s, social psychologist Walter Mischel headed several psychological studies on delayed rewards and gratification. He closely studied hundreds of children between the ages of 4 to 5 years to reveal a trait that is known to be one of the most important factors that determine success in a person's life, gratification.

This experiment is famously referred to as the marshmallow test. The experiment involved introducing every child into a private chamber and placing a single marshmallow in front of them. At this stage, the researcher struck a deal with the child.

The researcher informed them that he would be gone from the chamber for a while. The child was then informed that if he or she didn't eat the marshmallow while the researcher was away, he would come back and reward them with an additional marshmallow apart from the one on the table. However, if they did eat the marshmallow placed on the table in front of them, they wouldn't be rewarded with another.

It was clear. One marshmallow immediately or two marshmallows later.

The researcher walked out of the chamber and re-entered after 15 minutes.

Predictably, some children leaped on the marshmallow in front of them and ate it as soon as the researcher walked out of the room. However, others tried hard to restrain themselves by diverting their attention. They bounced, jumped around, and scooted on the chairs to distract themselves in a bid to stop them from eating the marshmallow. However, many of these children failed to resist the temptation and eventually gave in.

Only a handful of children managed to hold until the very end without eating the marshmallow.

The study was published in 1972 and became globally popular as 'The Marshmallow Experiment.' However, it doesn't end here. The real twist in the tale is what followed several years later.

Researchers undertook a follow-up study to track the life and progress of each child who was a part of the initial experiment. They studied several areas of the person's life and were surprised by what they discovered. The children who delayed gratification for higher rewards or waited until the end to earn two marshmallows instead of one had higher school grades, lower instances of substance abuse, lower chances of obesity, and better stress coping abilities.

The research was known as a ground-breaking study on gratification because researchers followed up on the children 40 years after the initial experiment was conducted, and it was sufficiently evident that the group of children who delayed gratification patiently for higher rewards succeeded in all areas they were measured on.

This experiment proved beyond doubt that delaying gratification is one of the most crucial skills for success in life.

Success and delaying gratification

Success usually boils down to picking between the discomfort of discipline over the pleasure and comfort of distraction. This is exactly what delaying gratification is. Would you rather go out for the new movie in town where all your friends are heading, or would you rather sit up and study for an examination to earn good grades? Would you rather party hard with your co-workers before the team gets started with an important upcoming presentation? Or would you sit late and work on fine tuning the presentation?

Our ability to delay gratification is also a huge factor when it comes to decision making and is considered an important aspect of emotional intelligence. Each day, we make several choices and decisions. While some are trivial and have little influence on our future (what color shoes should I buy? Or which way should I take to work?), others have a huge bearing on our success and future.

As human beings, we are wired to make decisions or choices that offer an instant return on investment. We want quick results, actions, and rewards. The mind is naturally tuned for a short-term profit. Why do you think e-commerce giants are making a killing by charging an additional fee for same day and next day delivery? Today is better than tomorrow!

Think about how different our life would be if we thought about the impact of our decisions about three to five years from now? If we can bring about this mental shift where we can delay gratification by keeping our eyes firmly fixated on the bigger picture several years from now, our lives can be very different.

Another factor that is important in gratification delay is the environment. For example, if children who were able to resist temptation were not given a second marshmallow or reward for delaying gratification, they are less likely to view delaying gratification as a positive habit.

If parents do not keep their commitment to reward a child for delaying gratification, the child won't value the trait. Delaying gratification can be picked up only in an environment of commitment and trust, where a second marshmallow is given when deserved.

Examples of gratification delay

Let us say you want to buy your dream car that you see in the showroom on your way to work every day. You imagine how wonderful it would be to own and drive that car. The car costs $25,000, and you barely have $5000 dollars in your current savings. How do you buy the car then? Simple, you start saving. This is how you will combine strong willpower with delayed gratification.

There are countless opportunities for you to blow money every day such as hitting the bar with friends for a drink on weekends, co-workers visiting the nearest coffee shop to grab a latte, or buying expensive gadgets. Every time you remove your wallet to pay, you have two clear choices: either blow your money on monetary pleasure or wait for the long-term reward. If you can resist these temptations and curtail your expenses, you'll be closer to purchasing your dream car. Making this decision will help you buy a highly desirable thing in future.

Will you spend now for immediate gratifications and pleasures, or will you save to buy something more valuable in the future?

Here is another interesting example to elucidate the concept of delayed gratification. Let us say you want to be the best film director the world has ever seen. You want to master the craft and pick up all skills related to movie making and the entertainment business. You visualize yourself as making spectacular movies that inspire and entertain people for decades.

How do you plan to work towards a large goal, or the big picture (well, literally)? You'll start by doing mundane, boring; uninspiring jobs on the sets such as being someone's assistant, fetching them a cup of coffee, cleaning the sets, and other similar boring chores. It isn't exciting or fun, but you go through it each day because you have your eyes firmly fixated on the larger goal, or bigger picture.

You know you want to become a huge filmmaker one day and are prepared to delay gratification for fulfilling that goal. The discomfort of your current life is smaller in comparison to the pleasure of the higher goal. This is delayed gratification. Despite the discomfort, you regulate your actions and behavior for meeting a bigger goal in the future. It may be tough and boring currently, but you know that doing these arduous tasks will give you that shot to make it big someday.

Delayed gratification can be applicable in all aspects of life from health to relationships. Almost every decision we make involves a decision between opting for short-term pleasures now and enjoying bigger rewards later. A burger can give you immediate pleasure today, whereas an apple may not give you instant pleasure but will benefit your body in the long run.

Stop drop technique

Each time you identify an overpowering or stressful emotion that is compelling you to seek immediate pleasure, describe your feelings by writing them down. Make sure you state them clearly to acknowledge their existence.

Have you seen the old VCR models? They had a big pause button prominently placed in the middle. You are now going to push the pause button on your thoughts.

Focus all attention on the heart as it is the center of all your feelings.

Think of something remarkably beautiful that you experienced. It can be a spectacular sunset you witnessed on one of your trips, a beautiful flower you saw in a garden today, or a cute pet kitten you spotted in the neighborhood. Basically, anything that evokes feelings of joy, happiness, and positivity in you. The idea is to bring about a shift in your feelings.

Experience the feeling for some time and allow it to linger. Imagine the feelings you experience in and around your heart. If it is still challenging, take deep breaths. Hold the positive feeling and enjoy it.

Now, click on the mental pause button and revisit the compelling idea that was causing stressful feelings. How does it feel right now?

Now write down how you are feeling and what comes to mind. Act on the fresh insight if it is suitable.

This process doesn't take much time (again, you are craving instant gratification) and makes it easier for you to resist giving in to temptation. The real trick is to change the physical feeling with the heart to bring about a shift in thoughts and eventually, actions. You don't suffocate or undermine your emotions.

Rather, you acknowledge them and then gently change them. When your emotions are slowly changing, the brain tows its line which makes us think in a way that lets us act according to our values and not on impulse or uncontrollable emotions.

Self-mastery is the master key

According to Walter Mischel, "Goal-directed and self-imposed gratification delay is fundamental to the process of emotional self-regulation." Emotional management, or regulation and the ability to control one's impulses, are vital to the concept of emotional intelligence.

Mischel's research established that while some people are born with a greater control for impulses, or better emotional management, others are not. A majority of people are somewhere in between. However, the good news is that emotional management, unlike intelligence, can be learned through practice. EQ isn't as genetically determined as cognitive abilities.

Impulse control and delayed gratification

Have you ever said something in anger and then regretted it immediately? Have you ever acted on an impulse or in haste only to regret it soon after the act? I can't even count the number of people who have lost their jobs, ruined their relationships, nixed their business negotiations, and blown away friendships because of that one moment when they acted on impulse. When you don't allow thoughts to take over and control your words or actions, you demonstrate low emotional intelligence.

Thus, the concept of emotional intelligence is closely connected with delaying gratification. We've all acted at some point or another without worrying about the consequences of our actions. Impulse control, or the ability to construct our thoughts and actions prior to speaking or acting, is a huge part of emotional control. You can manage your emotions more efficiently when you learn to override impulses, which is why impulse control is a huge part of emotional intelligence.

Ever wondered about the reason behind counting to ten, 100, or 1000 before reacting each time you are angry? We've all had our parents and educators counsel us about how anger can be restrained by counting up to ten or 100. It is simple, while you are in the process of counting; your emotional level is slowly decreasing. Once you are done with counting, the overpowering impulse to react to the emotion has passed. This allows you act in a more rational and thoughtful manner.

Emotional intelligence is about identifying these impulsive reactions and regulating them in a more positive and constructive manner. Rather than reacting mindlessly to a situation, you need to stop and think before responding. You choose to respond carefully instead of reacting impulsively to accomplish a more positive outcome or thwart a potentially uncomfortable situation.

Here are some useful tips for delaying gratification and boosting your ability to regulate emotions:

- Have a clear vision for your future

Delaying gratification and controlling impulses or emotions becomes easier when you have a clear picture of the future. When you know what you want to accomplish five, eight, ten, or 15 years from now, it will be a lot easier to keep the bigger picture in mind if you come across temptations that can ruin your goal. Your 'why' (compelling reason for accomplishing a goal) will keep you sustained throughout the process of meeting the goal. Have a plan to fulfill your goal once you have a clear goal in mind. Identifying your goals and planning how you'll get there will help you resist the temptation more effectively.

- Find ways to distract yourself from temptations and eliminate triggers

For instance, if you are planning to quit drinking, take a different route back home from work if there are several bars along the way. Instead of focusing on what you can't do, concentrate on the activities you are passionate about. Surround yourself with positive people and activities that will help you dwell on your goal. Avoid trying to fill your time with material goods.

- Make spending money difficult

If you are a slave to plastic money and online transactions, you are making the process of spending money too easy for your own good. Paying with cold, hard cash can make you think several times before spending. You'll reconsider your purchases when you pay with real money rather than plastic. Take a part of your salary and put it into a separate account that you won't touch. Make sure that accessing your savings account won't be easy.

- Avoid 'all or nothing' thinking

Most of us think resisting temptation or giving up a bad habit is an 'all or nothing challenge.' It is natural for a majority of normal human beings to have a minor slip here and there. However, that doesn't mean you should just fall off and quit. Occasional slip-ups shouldn't be used as an excuse to get off the track. Despite a small detour, you can get back on the track. Don't try to convince yourself to wander in the opposite direction.

- Make a list of common rationalizations

Find a counterpoint or counterargument for each. For example, you were angry for just five minutes, or you are spending only ten dollars extra. Tell yourself that five minutes of anger is 150 minutes a month wasted in anger or ten dollars extra is $3,000 extra spent throughout the year.

Chapter 2. Introduction to Meditation

It is widely believed that meditation is relaxation. However, relaxation is mere resting; it is the opposite of action. Meditation is not just resting, it is the dynamic state of pure consciousness from where wisdom and creativity originate.

In Japanese, there is a word called 'Mushin' which translates into 'no thought or emotion'. A warrior rises to this state when his moves in combat are no more a mechanical technique or an emotional expression but a spontaneous response to reality. Similarly, when we live with such spontaneity and deep awareness while seated or while in action; we are in meditation. There has been enough scientific study to prove that there is change in thought waves during meditation. Meditative waves are saner than the ones in our so called wakeful state.

Contemplation or concentration is also taught in the name of meditation. However, these are qualitatively different phenomena. Concentration is focusing on an object or activity and is a very deliberate phenomenon which is necessary in our day to day life. Contemplation means reflecting on a quality or an idea. It is more subtle than concentration and requires a mind which is calm and patient. One may contemplate on ideas of goodness, love and beauty but deliberation still exists.

Meditation is the state where the attention is free and no longer bound to an object or an idea. It is consciousness in its purest state. It is emptiness and receptivity. In this state, we receive wisdom from the unknown. We are aware but in a very calm way; without any effort. This happens to us many times a day between intervals of thoughts; but our thoughts are flowing so quickly that we cannot feel the gaps. That gap between two thoughts is when meditation takes place.

You would have noticed that energy flows through you in different ways. Angry energy is qualitatively different from happy energy. Excited and anxious energy is different from jealous energy. All these energies are carried by moods which are temporary and unwise. The meaning of meditative energy is your energy in its purest state, uncorrupted by moods and thought. This energy has an inherent quality of intelligence, creativity and bliss.

Many people associate meditation with escapism but it is the active people who benefit the most. It is the creation of supreme physical and mental health within us. A person who meditates inevitably excels in his work and is mysteriously supported by good fortune in important activities. It not only enhances one's aura, beauty and charm but also makes one's presence a matter of soulful joy for the people around.

Meditation enriches our life and protects us while we fulfill the purpose of our visit on Earth. It is the revelation of the pure being within us. Imagine there is a beautiful picture framed in your living room, covered with dust. You bring a cloth and clean the dust so that the picture is revealed in its true beauty. Similarly, meditation cleans the dust of unnecessary thoughts settled upon your mysterious being.

Meditation doesn't mean we would lose the capacity to think. In fact, the mind will be used more efficiently; like a smart phone uses an application. The phone does not need to keep playing the contents of an app continuously on the screen when the app is not in use. Similarly, we don't need to keep projecting thoughts on the screen of our mind when they are not needed. This is the reason why people fall in love with meditation. They experience a joy which has no cause; it's a sheer outpour of pure energy in their being.

Understanding Meditation

"Once meditation gains flow, your very energy will be your armor."

How to meditate? It is very important to understand that meditation is a natural process, like sunrise and sunset. It is just like breathing, like a flower blossoming. Do we have to go and open the petals of a bud so that it can blossom? If we did so, we would only ruin its growth. When we are trying to meditate with techniques, we are trying to pull out the petals of our consciousness.

A question naturally comes to the mind, "Then what is one supposed to do?"

The state of meditation is not happening within us often, because we are constantly absent to reality. It is difficult to realize and even more difficult to accept that most of our actions are a series of mechanical responses devoid of true presence. Simple activities like cleaning the room, working in office, drinking tea, talking, listening, cooking, eating, etc. can lead to meditation if we add to them the quality of our presence and vitality. Action becomes meditation if we are present in the act; thoughts disappear and joy is revealed. Unnecessary thoughts are the result of incomplete actions and desires. When each act is total, there is natural fulfillment and no need for thought to dream. This is as far as activity is concerned. To balance continuous activity, let us sit in meditation once or twice every day. If our activities are meditative, the sitting sessions will be brimming with wisdom and joy. All senses and thoughts will move towards silence. Just as awareness is needed in activity, patience is needed in sitting sessions.

These two qualities hold the secret key to the growth and understanding of meditation: Our presence in action and patience in stillness.

Both aspects of your life, activity and inactivity will complement each other to take you into mysterious and nourishing realms of meditation.

When someone tells you that you have to spend years to learn meditation or to be spiritual, know that he doesn't know. Meditation is always in the 'now'. It is we who are not able to stop clinging to our thoughts and habits. This life is so intelligently created that we cannot deceive it. Our mind can't be quiet until we are holding on to habits and rigid beliefs. Hence, it takes years and lifetimes to create space within, where boundaries can dissolve and bliss can grow.

Every day, I go for long walks wherever I am staying. I wander in the woods rather than walking in circles in a park. When I am in Mumbai, walking means making way through traffic until one reaches a quiet spot. Earlier, my friends who didn't enjoy walking would get confused seeing me stroll aimlessly and would ask me the purpose of my long walks. I would have no answer as I walk for the fun of it and not for any benefit. Now these very friends have started walking in the park because of cholesterol problems. With great willpower they reach the park on their motorbikes before they commence walking in circles. Very few people walk for the love of it. Same is the case with meditation. People want to meditate for the benefits. They keep moving in circles. If we meditate for the love of it, meditation would be like wandering in the woods and sometimes walking through the city's madness. Health and happiness would be as natural as breathing.

When you were born as a child, you had no identity. The first thing added to you was your name. When that name was continuously repeated and as the senses gained authority, it finally got etched within that you and others were separate. Experiences of pleasure, pain, relationships, fear, pride, etc. were added later to memory. All these memories came together to create a person that is you. Isn't it so?

Meditation is once again being innocent and blissful like a child. That is what we essentially are. When unnecessary thoughts and emotions are like dry leaves falling from the tree, this happens by itself. The urge to meditate has to be total and uncorrupted by pleasure or fear. This urge is as natural to our being as the urge to eat when the body needs food.

This journey has many a beautiful stops but there is no destination. Meditation is the art of forgetting. It is cutting the roots of all unnecessary concerns and being in the moment. Right now, if you trust life totally wherever it may lead you, you will rise out of all your concerns like a hot air balloon going upwards, like an eagle gliding in the sky. There can be no 'one formula suits all' method for meditation. It is very important that we listen to our inner wisdom at every turn of life.

Many may ask, 'What about our daily struggle? We have to live in this world as responsible sons, daughters, husbands, wives, employees, employers, businessmen, citizens and so on. How will meditation help us in our practical lives?'

Once meditation gains flow, your very energy will be your armor. You will see that your problems are melting without any stress on your own part. You will inevitably perform the right actions; unknowingly plant the right seeds in your worldly life. People will perceive you in a different light. Relationships will become more real, creative and beautiful. This phenomenon which is called 'Grace' by religions is simply our connection with the omnipresent cosmic energy, the source of all generosity and abundance. Meditative energy is a self-perpetuating energy. Just as our body has the intelligence to create comfort and safety for itself anywhere, this energy creates the required surroundings in which it can grow and flower.

What's required on our part is to be generous to our own intelligence. To be ready to go a mile into the dark, knowing nothing but feeling something, waiting for our eyes to get adjusted to darkness. We will then realize that the moon is ever shining within, leading us towards right action.

The Atmosphere Of Meditation

"Realization triggers a passion which sets us free from all things unnecessary."

We understand by now, that meditation is a natural process. When everything within becomes quiet and still, the boundaries created by thought disappear. This disappearance of boundaries is the dissolving of the individual into the divine. When a guest is expected by us, don't we clear the junk in our house for it to be neat and tidy? We rearrange all the misplaced things so that there is order and beauty. Similarly, we need to prepare our hearts to host the divine by casting away all the activities which cause negativity in our life.

Suppose you are an artist, a painter. Would you stand in the rain to paint your picture? The rain would undoubtedly undo the picture you are trying to paint. Would you plant a sapling in the middle of a football ground? The inner world too unveils itself when there is care taken to protect its vibrations. Meditative energy is the purest form of our consciousness. We need to be mindful in our daily lives so that this energy continuously grows and spreads its beauty in each area of our life. We are carrying the precious seed of meditation within us; we must be careful about what we eat, what we do, what we say and which feelings we nurture within us. Since meditation is cessation of disturbance, we must try to avoid everything that creates disturbance in the harmony of our life.

Imposed discipline is insufficient for the creation of harmony. The most effective way is to be observant in our actions and to be sensitive to all that we consume in the form of food, intoxication and entertainment. If we observe ourselves closely even for seven days, we will realize that many of our actions are harmful for our own happiness. Simple things like the quality of feelings we carry for our friends and loved ones, the way we talk to certain people; just observing keenly is enough. We can also immediately sense it when we are overindulging in certain things. We can be aware of our thought processes, which are continuously projecting us into the future and throwing us into the past. If we watch closely, we will inevitably realize that our energies are being trapped by certain feelings, thoughts, fears and habits. Realization triggers a passion which sets us free from all things unnecessary.

Have you ever noticed how birds make their nests? With such precision and energy they instinctively choose the contents which will be the first home for their young ones. It is like these birds that we must act for the growth of our being. We are blessed not only with instinct but also with intuition. Clear cut do's and don'ts are good for the worldly affairs but deep understanding is required for this divine affair.

Numerous gifts are added to our personality throughout the journey of meditation. A meditative person inevitably seems attractive to fellow people and is a guide to the ones who are seeking higher states of consciousness. He or she becomes a magnet to good fortune and inner riches. We shouldn't get carried away by misunderstanding gifts as achievements. Humility is like a shield in the inside world. Humility does not just mean behaving meekly; it means staying with the unknown when one is seduced by sweet but limited images of oneself. When we give attention to things which are unnecessary our energies become feeble. Humility is to stay in innocence and not to let the sublime flow of wisdom degrade into gross knowledge. It is letting pride slip over oneself like a dewdrop over a leaf.

Another value which is of great importance in the inner realm is 'sensitivity'. It is both; a gift and a virtue. Sensitivity is the capacity to understand and feel reality beyond the self. It is the knack of forgetting ourselves and perceiving with love, the life around us. Perception expands as sensitivity grows. We begin to understand certain things instantly; things that we could not grasp before, even after hours of deliberation. One day in a sensitive person's life is of more value than a hundred days lived by a person whose heart is dull. However, the kind of crass entertainment and media we nowadays devour is destroying our sensitivity with time. It is just like consuming drugs. When a person begins to take drugs, one shot is enough to give a high. However, as time goes by, the body becomes tolerant and the person requires a stronger dose to get the same high. Our brain becomes duller as we overindulge in pleasures which are not artistic but simplistic.

When one goes into meditation, one becomes immensely sensitive. The consciousness which was busy with thoughts is once again pure and free to feel the environment. Many people wonder what the use of meditation is, if it's making a person more sensitive to the environment. Meditative people don't prefer strong sensations, loud noise, harsh talking, etc. People assume that this is a weakness. However, they don't understand that meditation is an art. Just like an artist has a certain sense of aesthetics, a meditative person has certain sense when it comes to the realm of consciousness. A good musician is not good because he can tolerate loud music, he is good because he can understand and create quality music. Similarly, a meditative person is not one who can bear unintelligent vibes but the one who can create a pure blissful atmosphere without recourse to crude pleasure.

Meditation and sensitivity help each other to blossom. Just as hummingbirds spread the pollen of the flower they feed on, sensitivity spreads the seeds of meditation. It gives hints and directions to our actions. If we act according to these hints, we undoubtedly progress in meditation. If one values sensitivity, a miracle happens. Suddenly, the one who was seeking pleasure becomes the source of joy to oneself and others. The one who was restless and bored becomes creative. And as this sensitivity grows within our hearts, it leads us into the very bosom of life where fear, suffering and isolation disappear.

The Basics Of Meditation

Chakra Healing Meditation

When healing your chakras, it is important to start at the root and work your way up rather than working from the top down.

Begin by focusing all of your energy at the base of your spine. Breathe in and out as you continue to feel this in your body. Each part of your body should be relaxed in this moment.

Start by making sure that you are not holding on to any tension in your legs or your arms. Our chests and our stomach can also stay rather tight from all the tension. Breathe in as you fill yourself with positivity and breathe out any of the tension that you are still holding within these different parts. Your root chakra is also known as your Muladhara.

Your root chakra will deal with different aspects of your career. Money and mindset are also involved in this. Anything that deals with your overall survival will be located within this root chakra. If you are struggling with your career, monetary issues, or anything else that creates the life that you have, then this could be creating a blockage in your root chakra. The worst possible thing for this root chakra is fear.

When you are holding on to that anxiety and stress, no matter what it might be over, then it will be found within the blockage passageways of your root chakra.

Breathe in positivity and allow this part of yourself to become clean. Any part of your overall foundation of life needs to be healed within this moment. Let yourself be as grounded as possible.

Breathe in for one, two, three, four, and five. Breathe out for five, four, three, two, and one.

Become independent from your financial state. This does not determine who you are as a person. Having a lot of money or having no money at all will create a very different lifestyle. The only people who say that money isn't everything are those that already have money. Money can provide you, not with happiness, but with the relief and the security needed in order to actually explore that happiness. What we have to remember is that regardless of our financial state, we are still living, breathing individuals. We still have needs, wants, and desires. There are greater things in life than seeking out money. Of course, you need to have money in order to pay for basic living expenses. But beyond that, we do not need money to provide us with any sort of fulfillment. Let yourself become free from this type of stress.

Remind yourself that work is not everything, either. Many people will believe that their job is their life, but you have so much more to live for aside from just this. Feel at the bottom of your spine and all throughout your legs as your root chakra becomes released. The stress and the fear will only make this worse. Of course, you will not be free from the worry over money, but you do not have to let that panic get to a level where it is causing a blockage of your energy. Breathe in positivity and happiness and breathe out anything that is keeping you restricted here. Let's move up now to our sacral chakra. This is known as your Svadhishthana.

This chakra deals with pleasure. Anything associated with sexuality will be found within this energy center as well.

Your sacral chakra is located in your lower abdomen. You can feel where your belly button is now and know that around two or three inches beneath this is where you will discover your sacral chakra. Anything dealing with your guilt or worry over your relationships, could be found here.

If you have an indulgence, or a lack of pleasure, this could create a certain problem in your life. The desire and seeking of too much pleasure can be a distraction. Everyone deserves to have fun, but it can quickly become an addiction.

Consider now if you have been over indulgent with anything. Even food could be a form of addiction or release that is helping you to avoid emotional problems you don't want to confront. Feel yourself become released from this now.

Sexuality is another huge part of the energy that makes up your sacral chakra. Have you been experiencing difficulties with your sexual life? Is there a partner that you have been having problems with? Do you feel as though this area of your life is lacking anything substantial? Breathe in positivity and breathe out any of the blockages that are keeping your sacral chakra from having the ability to completely heal. Breathe in and out, in and out. Moving up is our solar plexus chakra. This is referred to as your Manipura.

Your solar plexus chakra deals with your own personal power. Breathe in for one, two, three, four, and five. Breathe out for five, four, three, two, and one.

This is your willpower and the motivation that you have within. Can you be confident and in control of your life? This ability will be discovered within that location on your body. It is essential that we ensure we are not putting any blockages or negativity into our own ability to have this kind of power.

This solar plexus chakra is located above your belly button and just below your chest, in the stomach area. This is where you will experience butterflies in your stomach when you know that something is wrong. This is where that big heavy ball will be. When something is making you nervous or giving you an unsteady feeling, then you might discover that pit in your stomach. This is your solar plexus chakra telling you that you need to take control. If you feel any sort of shame over yourself, or embarrassment about who you are, this will be a huge blockage. You cannot properly make positive decisions for yourself when this solar plexus chakra is being blocked. You need to have that belief and that strength in your own abilities so that you can live to your fullest potential.

Breathe in positivity and breathe out anything that has been blocking this part of your body. Your self-worth will also be regulated by the energy that exists here. Your self-esteem is an important part as well and you need to be able to nurture that so that you can make better decisions. Loving yourself and fulfilling your needs of having a high self-esteem is healthy and it does not make you egotistical; we need to check in with ourselves so that we can be our own biggest fan. Breathe in and out. Breathe in self-love and breathe out any of the hate and doubt that has been keeping this part of your chakras blocked.

Moving up we have our heart chakra. This is the chakra that deals with everything involving love and relationships. This energy does not just regulate personal relationships with other people. It is also responsible for helping you control the love that you have for yourself.

Any sort of grief or remorse will be the biggest blockage for this part of your heart chakra. It is located right in between your breasts in that deep part of your chest. It is also known as the Anahata.

Any type of joy or inner peace that you experience will be found in this part of your body. Your heart might beat faster when you are happier. Your heart may be heavy when you are unsure of yourself and you don't know what to do. This will all be part of the regulation of your heart chakra.

Breathe in happiness and breathe out hate. Fill yourself up with peace and let go of any of the grief or shame that you might be feeling. Let yourself heal from the emotional trauma and relationships with romantic people that might have been causing you this sort of blockage. Breathe in positivity and breathe out anything that is keeping you restricted.

Above this is our throat chakra. This is located right in your throat. It is also referred to as Vishuddha. This throat chakra is all about communication. Look at your life now and the way that you have been talking and interacting with other people. Do you share the things that are on your mind? Are you not afraid to stand up for what you know is right and true?

If you are telling lies, or speaking hateful things, this will block your throat chakra. Your expression is important, but you also have to look at the way that the negative things that you share don't just affect other people but also cause anguish in your life. It takes a lot of energy to send negativity to somebody else.

It fills you with hate when you spread that to somebody else. Open your mouth wide now and breathe in as big of a breath as you can. Feel yourself fill with positive air.

Hold it for just a few moments and now exhale as hard as you can, letting go of all of that hate that you have been sending to other people. Feel yourself become lifted and free once you let go of all that toxic energy that is being passed around. Your throat chakra can also be blocked when you are not properly using it. Are you more of a passive person who isn't willing to share what is on their mind? This is only going to keep your throat chakra closed off even more. Open this part of yourself up and let yourself communicate with other people. Breathe in and out, in and out. Let yourself be at peace.

Moving up to the middle of our forehead, we have our third-eye chakra. This is known as your Ajna.

Your third-eye chakra is your intuition. It is something that will help lead you through this life. Not everybody will be able to even tap into their third-eye chakra in their life, even when they already know that it exists. You have to allow yourself to see the truth. Sometimes we know that the truth is right in front of us, but we keep that third-eye closed because we're not ready to look at it. Open this up now and be honest with yourself. Once you relieve this blockage, you will find that every other chakra aligns. Once you stop looking the other way with your third-eye and instead look right in front of you, this is going to help keep your body at peace and bring everything together in perfect harmony.

Breathe in and out, in and out. Your imagination, your creativity, your wisdom, and your logical thinking all exists within this third-eye as well. Any sort of illusion or deceit that you have been experiencing, or even creating on your own, is going to be a huge blockage for this third-eye chakra.

Feel your eyes become open. See the things that are right in front of you. Close your eyes once again and breathe in. You do not have to use your physical set of eyes to really let this third-eye breathe. Let the air travel in and out. Breathe in positivity and truth and breathe out any sort of neglect that you have had over your life.

On top of all of these chakras finally is our crown chakra. This is known as your Sahasrara.

Your crown chakra represents how connected you can be to your spirituality, regardless of whatever you might believe in this life. You have something deeper inside of you that extends beyond just your physical body. Allow this crown chakra to be your guidance. Feel this take power over you and let it be the thing that drives the rest of your chakras. Trust your intuition. Let yourself speak your truth. Feel and spread the love. Trust your gut and know when something is right or wrong. Allow yourself to feel pleasure but remember that it can't be everything. Keep yourself grounded and rooted in this earth and the present moment. The only way that you can heal is after you have managed to clean these out. Think of a physical wound that you might get. If you were to scrape your knee, before putting ointment or a bandage on it to heal, you first need to make sure that it is clean. If you are not properly cleaning something out first, then it could trap something negative or toxic inside of it, which would cause it to spread everywhere else and get even worse than it was before the initial wound.

You have cleaned your chakras, and you have granted yourself the ability to fully heal, breathe in and out, in and out. You are completely at peace; your chakras have aligned, and you know now what it takes to feel at ease. You are relaxed and you are mindful.

You are present in this moment and you are prepared. You are peaceful and serene.

You are now completely relaxed and at ease. You have tapped into every one of your chakras. You know where they exist inside of you now and it is time to start the healing process. You'll be able to go back to this whenever you need to ensure that you don't have any blockages.

This is the perfect beginner and warm-up meditation because it means that you will be able to go through the rest of these meditations with a clear mind and a healthy flow through your body. Continue to focus on your breathing once again. Breathe in for one, two, three, four, and five, and out for five, four, three, two, and one.

Feel yourself already start to heal in this process. Allow your body to become calm and centered.

We are going to count down from twenty once again. When we reach one, you will either drift off to sleep, continue on with your day, or move onto the next meditation.

Breathe in for five and out for five.

Types Of Techniques Of Meditation

There are many different types and techniques of meditation that we shall not be able to cover everything. Meditative techniques are in the hundreds but are all linked by the common thread of aiming at achieving inner peace for the practitioner.

First and foremost, all meditative practices engage in mind-control techniques as a way to achieve relaxation and peace. Second, there are postures and body movements that are found in all forms of meditation. These two traits are evident in all meditative practices pointing to a common goal for all of them.

Meditation helps to relieve our bodies and minds of the toxic effects of stress. It relaxes us and brings the peace of mind that we all yearn for. Before you pick up one form of meditation or another, it is important to do your research and learn as much as you can about them. Interrogate yourself. Find out and decide what your meditative goals are or would be to help you pick up the right technique for you.

In some cases, you will need to get a teacher or join a meditation school for the right advice, coaching, and mentorship in taking up meditation. There are types of meditative practices that cannot be performed by beginners, people with certain conditions or illnesses, or older people, for example. Seeking the right information will guide you to the right technique. You must take on a meditative practice that will fit your lifestyle. Meditation requires consistency, regularity, discipline, and high commitment for one to realize the desired fruits. With the many types of meditation in existence, we can generally categorize meditation as follows:

Concentrative Meditation: In concentrative meditation, the mind is directed to a particular object, chant/mantra, sound, or sensation. The practitioner will focus their mind and energy on a focal point of their choosing that best works for them to clear and calm their minds and bodies. This type of meditation is good for beginners.

Mindfulness Meditation: This type of meditation does not rely on focusing the mind on an object but relies on feelings, sensations, emotions and thought patterns to achieve a meditative state. These are more advanced types of meditation that are not for everyone, especially beginners:

Buddhist Meditation: Zen Meditation (Zazen): Zazen is Japanese meaning "seated Zen" or "seated meditation," referring to the form of Zen meditation practiced while sitting. Zazen originates from Chinese Zen Buddhism. It is done while seated on the floor, usually on a mat, with crossed legs. This was traditionally done in the lotus or half-lotus position.

For the mind, Zazen employs two techniques:

- Focus on breathing. The practitioner will pay attention to the inhalation and exhalation while silently counting down with every breath and back.
- Shikantanza. Here, there is no specific object of meditation. One remains in the moment being aware of what goes through their mind and what passes around.
- Vipassana Meditation: Vipassana means clear seeing or insight and is a Buddhist type of meditation. It is ideal for mental discovery and awareness. It starts with mindfulness of breath to stabilize and focus the mind (focused-mind meditation), then it moves to develop clarity of awareness of bodily sensations and mental phenomena. Sit on the floor, legs crossed, with a straight back.

Mindfulness Meditation: Mindfulness meditation combines practices from various Buddhist meditation practices. It is widely employed in hospitals and other health benefits as a form of treatment. Here, the practitioner will focus on the moment while not losing awareness of thoughts and emotions experienced.

Religious/Spiritual Meditation. These are meditative practices that are practiced among different religions. Remember that spirituality is one avenue for achieving peace of mind and relaxation. Here, meditation and prayer are combined to achieve spiritual development by the reflection of God's Word.

Meditation is a communion with the self with the aim of spiritual development or divinity.

Meditation in religion is practiced for peace of mind by steadying and focusing it to give the practitioner the ability for divine insight. A practitioner of Christian meditation said that God is sought through the study of scripture, but through meditation, He is found. There are forms of meditative practices in almost all religions, which prove the close link between spirituality and meditation.

Sufism meditative practices are some of the most elaborate of religious meditation. Practitioners get into a rhythm of chanting and movement that eventually transports participants into a spiritual realm. In Christianity, there are examples with the Catholics and Orthodox sects that have mantras or repetitive prayers.

Metta Meditation. It is also referred to as loving-kindness meditation and has its roots in Tibet. This meditative form enhances empathy and compassion to make one more loving to self and others. The practitioner will sit and close their eyes, then generate feelings of kindness and compassion in their mind toward themselves then progress to others. Just like the name suggests, this type of meditation aims at creating harmony with one's surroundings. Treat all things with kindness, and the rewards are happiness and compassion for you. You emit happiness, and the world bounces it back to you.

Hindu Meditations: Vedic and Yogic forms of meditation are Hindu forms and are classified as follows:

Mantra Meditation. Mantra involves the repetition of a word or phrase to focus on one's mind.

Transcendental Meditation. Transcendental techniques aim at opening the mind.

Yoga Meditation. Yoga means "union," and it has many types. Yoga combines mind relaxing and focusing on practices with stretching movements and postures. Of all the meditative practices, yoga is the most popular of the secular forms of meditation and has the most following for nonreligious or spiritual meditation. You will find that most people who meditate are practicing one form of yoga or another.

How then do we use these techniques for self-improvement and relaxation? Let us first know the benefits of meditation.

Benefits Of Meditation

Meditation is an easy method to quiet your mind, to relax, and to escape the stress of daily life. It does not require advanced techniques to learn. Meditation doesn't even require long hours to master. Quite simply, meditation allows you to calm down, to relax, and to gain insight.

Meditation involves quieting the constant babble of our thoughts. This sounds simple, but it's not. Right now, stop thinking for ten seconds. You'll find yourself thinking about those ten seconds and why you're supposed to stop thinking. It's natural for our minds to question and to analyze. Even when we sleep, our brains are active. Our bodies may be resting, but dreams are proof that our minds are not quiet. Meditation lets the body AND mind relax. When that happens, we gain a peaceful experience of calm and insight.

Some methods of meditation try to trick the mind into becoming quiet. The Zen method asks meditators to ponder an idea that doesn't make sense. The mind tries, tries again, and then stops and is quiet. The Zen question "What is the sound of one hand clapping?" is an example. One hand can't clap, so there is no sound. But if one hand tries to clap, what is produced?

The problem with the Zen technique is our thoughts. We give up pondering the question and begin thinking again. We might think "This was silly;" we might remember the grocery list. And so our quiet mind doesn't last. But there are ways to avoid letting the mind keep thinking. They are simple and can be done at any time you have a few minutes free. Have fun!

Studies have documented the medical benefits of meditation. You can explore these in depth by searching "Meditation" on the internet. Meditation reduces stress, which contributes to disease, to unhappiness, and often leads to alcohol or chemical abuse.

Portions of the brain influence us in different ways. Our advanced abilities, such as art appreciation or math problem solving, are higher functions. But our brains control us physically and affect how we function. Basic core responses, such as fear and anger, are controlled by a primal center, nicknamed the "lizard brain" by psychologists. These emotions trigger a shutdown of more advanced brain functions. That way, our entire attention is channeled into a survival mode. In psychological terminology, when we are faced with danger or stress, we enter a "fight or flight" response. Our minds are not capable of deep reasoning when the brain feels under attack. In its defensive mode, our brain has readied the body for the dangers ahead. In early days, men might have been attacked by a beast. They had to determine whether to run from the beast or fight it.

These days we rarely react to a stressor by fighting. We also don't run away physically. But our bodies react as though we might. Adrenalin floods our system. It remains, as does our stress, as we experience the reaction. Since we don't need to fight or flee, the adrenalin is not required or used. Our brains don't realize the emergency is over, so the small lizard brain still overrides our higher reasoning. We can't reason away stress as a result, just as we can't tell the brain to be quiet.

But meditation gives us a method to remove the stress and mess of "fight or flight." It helps the mind bypass the issue by working at the deep core to calm us. Once that happens, our higher mental functions return. And if we keep working with meditating, we maintain our healthy state. It won't prevent stress from occurring in our lives. But instead of dwelling on it, we can calm ourselves and can see the issue in a calm and holistic manner. Although we can't change how our brains react to outside events, we can adjust how our bodies handle the situation

It sounds so helpful that it must be difficult, like advanced yoga or tai chi. But there are no movements to practice or postures to assume. All you do is relax and let your mind relax too. Meditation has been around for centuries or even longer, although not always called meditation. It is simple. It works. All you have to do is try it. So now, here's an easy way to do that.

There are several benefits apart from the ones we have discussed in the preceding sections. It is no wonder then that meditation is being promoted as an alternative to clinical treatment for the cure and management of several health conditions and general wellbeing. Meditation leads the body to change. Cells in the body are injected with more energy resulting in peace, happiness, and motivation as the energy levels in the body are boosted.

Below are the benefits of meditative practices:

- Meditation reverses or reduces the production of stress hormones (adrenaline) by creating calmness and eradicating anxiety to prevent chronic stress. With controlled or regulated stress hormones, the body is more relaxed.

- It is good for managing blood pressure and other heart diseases or conditions since the heart rate and breathing are slowed down. When we are not stressed, worried, or anxious, the heart rate is slow; therefore, the blood pressure is also low. Meditation can help greatly with conditions like high blood pressure since it works to create calmness and relaxation.

- Boosts the immune system and slows aging as a result of less production of adrenaline by the body. The immune system is boosted since one ends up being healthier as a result of the suppression of destructive stress chemicals.

- Meditation brings clarity of the mind, and creativity is enhanced. With a relaxed mind, one is sure to be more creative and productive.

- Meditative techniques advocate for a pure life, and in fact, meditation aims to attain purity akin to the higher being, so practitioners find themselves quitting poisonous habits, like smoking, drug abuse, and alcohol consumption.

- Brain functioning is greatly improved through the boosting of psychological creativity, a better memory, and a settled, relaxed mind.

- Meditation makes you happier since your mind and body feel better. A relaxed person has no worries and will be a happier person.

- You will sleep better since you are relaxed, enabling you to have more rest and better rest to face the day and tasks that you are faced with.

- Meditation reduces how fast we age through mental and physical exercise. People who meditate have a slower aging process. Stress hormones hasten aging while meditation is known to halt or significantly reduce their production.

- Meditation reduces or eliminates stress. Meditation practice is a calm and happy individual who is essentially immune to the effects of stress.

- A relaxed and happier person has the benefit of a better functioning body. Immunity is boosted, and diseases are kept at bay.

- When one embraces meditation with all its tenets and understands it, they hold life to a greater value since they learn the true meaning and purpose of living.

- Meditative exercises improve metabolism and help regulate weight by fighting obesity.

- Meditation helps you feel more connected and in tune with yourself.

- Meditation brings emotional balance and harmony.

- Personal transformation is inevitable with meditation. You end up being a new person.

It is recommended that you meditate at least once a day for optimal results. Dawn meditation is highly recommended usually between 3:00 a.m. and 6:00 a.m. Dawn meditation is considered more beneficial as you tend to be more alert and well-rested after your sleep. The environment is also quiet and ideal for meditation. In the next part, we shall learn how to use meditation to reduce stress in your life.

Exercises

Do physical activity

The definition of physical activity in this context has not been limited only to exercise. Physical activity is any activity that engages your physique. Mostly it will lead to perspiration. When an individual engages in physical activity, he or she is obliged to concentrate fully on that particular activity. Exercising is a very renowned way to counter depression. Regular exercise has time and again been used as an anti-depressant. When one is exercising, endorphins are boosted. These are chemicals that enable an individual to feel good.

The statistics of how many people deal with stress is always on the upward. When one experiences stress, it has a lasting effect in their lives since it cuts across what an individual is engaging in at a particular time. To eradicate stress completely is an uphill task, and one would rather manage it. Exercising is one of the best methods to manage stress. Many medical practitioners advise that individuals should engage in exercises in a bid to manage stress levels.

The advantages that come with a person engaging in exercises have far been established to be a counter-measure against diseases and as a method of enhancing the body's physical state. Research has it that exercising helps a great deal when decreasing fatigue and enhancing the body's consciousness to the environment. Stress invades the whole of your body, affecting both the body and mind. When this happens, the act of your mind feeling well will be pegged on the act of the body feeling well too. When one is in the act of exercising, the brain produces endorphins which act naturally as pain relievers. They also improve the instances upon which an individual falls asleep. When the body is able to rest, this means that its amounts of anxiety have dropped by a large margin. Production of endorphins can also be triggered by the following practices. They include but are not limited to meditation and breathing deeply. Participation in exercise regularly has proven an overall tension reliever.

Doing relaxation exercises

Another method of reducing stress levels is through the use of some relaxation techniques. A relaxation technique is any procedure that is of aid to an individual when trying to calm down the levels of anxiety. Stress is effectively conquered when the body itself is responding naturally to the stress levels in the body. Relaxation can be often confused with laying on a couch after a hard day. This relaxation is best done in the form of self-meditation, although its effects are not fulfilling on the impact of stress. Most relaxation techniques are done at the convenience of your home with only an app.

Settling on the right technique for relieving stress is not easy. It is key that you focus on one that is not only favorable to your lifestyle but also your budget. There are various techniques for mind relaxation, which are:

Deep breathing

When breathing deeply, one increases the neuron-transmitters known as endorphins that seek to bring about a feeling of easiness. This technique forms the basis for other types of techniques. In order to achieve this, one needs to sit in a posture that allows his or her back to be straight. One hand should be firmly placed on the chest and the other on the stomach. An individual should inhale through the nostrils and exhale through the mouth. This procedure should be carried out cyclically and repetitive.

Continuous muscle relaxation

This happens in a two-phase kind of arrangement in that there are the contraction and relaxation of muscles. One phase entails tensing the muscles while the other involves relaxing them. This type of stress reliever works best when you ascend all the way up from your legs. Normally you should have lost clothing on with no shoes. You should take your time to practice the shifts in breathing. Commence with your right foot then your left making sure that you feel every moment of it. The movement should be in ascension, making sure you touch every muscle in your body.

Meditation

While in the process of meditation, make sure that you go through your whole body in your mind.

This will automatically assume an ascension kind of manner. Make sure that you face upwards with your legs separated. Focus on every particular part of your body, taking note of the different reactions that you are feeling. After going through your body, take some time to relax in a mode of doing nothing.

Vision of peace

Our eyes need to be shut during this particular exercise. Here, you close your eyes and see yourself in a state that is devoid of any technicalities. You need to see yourself in a place where you are enjoying yourself to the fullest. Experience peace at its peak. Enjoy the surrounding, for instance, the clean air, the warm sun rays, the friendly water. Feel as your anxiety drifts away, leaving you at peace. After that, you can then open your eyes gently and come back to real facts.

Calculated movements

Like meditation, exercising the mind through calculated movements entails engaging the mind on the events of the present. Whereas meditation focuses on the past, exercising the mind is akin to the current situations. Take, for instance, yoga or the famous Tai chi. These movements are done in a synchronized manner, one that enables the mind to relax. When the mind is relaxing, levels of stress fall.

Write

Writing is one of the many solutions to stress relief. Writing helps reduce stress levels to individuals with anxiety disorders since jotting down your horrible experiences is one way of parting with them completely. The type of writing that focuses on the previous events that might have taken place in the life of a person is referred to as writing in the form of expression. This is because the writer is trying to connect with the readers through opening up to them, telling them what he or she has been through. This type of writing may not be effective for every individual. Some individuals may be inclined to be haunted over and over again by what they are writing. This may cause more harm than good. With writing, one tends to evaluate the situation in different ways despite the outcome.

Apart from writing as a form of expression, there is another form of writing which entails that you write from a reflective point of view. With this type of view, an individual is able to visualize the situation differently. With this kind of writing, the writer is able to unearth various things that he or she had not put into consideration. With writing, it can be so confidential that an individual is able to write what he or she is ashamed of saying out to other people. People who write about particular events in their lives are the ones that spearhead the solution process.

Managing time in the right way for you

Here stress levels are brought about by timelines that we seek to meet in order to fulfill our obligations. All around the world, we are defined by the various responsibilities that are tied to us by the inherent nature of existence. Some of us are parents, and at the same time, have demanding jobs in a bid to make ends meet. Juggling between being a parent and being apt at your place of work is not an easy task. It will always leave you worn out if not stressed.

The old saying that time is money has never been side-shadowed at any ounce. The kind of life that an individual is leading will always be defined by the kind of life that a particular individual is leading. How best an individual manages time determines the degree of how best an individual leads his or her life. For instance, it is common sense that the body needs to rest in order to rejuvenate. To do this, the body requires at least eight hours to seven hours of sleep.

Meditate

This refers to a state of relating to your conscience. Meditation happens in your mind. These are usually episodes whereby one takes time to visualize what is happening in his or her life and trying to influence it positively. Meditation acts as a stress reliever since it influences the secretion of a neuron-transmitter known as endorphin that has a calming effect on the body.

Spend time with animals

Research has it that interacting with pets, or friendly animals have a calming effect on the levels of stress that an individual has. Research has it that most mental illnesses have been curbed by pets. Co-habiting with a pet comes with a bag of goodies that include uncompromised companionship. A pet will always be there by your side even when you are feeling lonely; the feeling will be eradicated.

Pets have time and again been used as a means of getting to know each other and making friends. With a pet in place, you are inclined to form social networks that will help you connect with other people regularly. With pets around, one's blood pressure is reduced to manageable levels; your overall cardiovascular health is improved. With a pet running here and there, we will always be obliged to exercise often when playing with them. When interacting with a pet, you feel like you are having a conversation with a normal human being. This, in turn, has two effects. First is that we will not experience loneliness. We will also be inclined to forget about the worse thoughts rather than dwelling on them.

Stay in the open air

The breathing of fresh air has a lot of positive effects on our bodies. Our bodies depend on the process of breathing in order to live progressively. Having a feel of clean air or a sensation of petals aids in the alleviation of stress. The levels of serotonin produced in the body are affected by the amounts of oxygen in the body. A higher level of serotonin leads to a hyped feeling of being amazed. For instance, the sensation found in lavender aids in the reduction of insomnia. Jasmine plant, on the other hand, has been used as a boost to mood.

Research has it that failure of exposure to clean air can be a cause of death. This was after a report was released with individuals succumbing to death due to polluted air. Fresh air enhances strength in the body. The respiration process that occurs in the production of energy has it that oxygen is a raw material. Fatigue comes as a result of not being exposed to fresh air for long periods of time.

Digestion is also a key aspect when it comes to fresh air. Taking a stroll allows the body to engage in a series of reactions that will enhance the digestion to take place faster. This is opposed to the habit of eating at your office desk as you continue with your task. The digestion here is curtailed, and thus, it affects the concentration levels of a particular individual. This person is obliged not to function for a longer period without getting fatigued.

The open-air exposes our lungs to fresh air. Smoking darkens our lungs and puts us at danger of cancer. The sensation of clean air in our lungs is relieving in the sense that you are feeling every part of your air sacks. This also aids in the eradication of sputum from our chests that will, in turn, lead to blockages.

Research has it that exposure to clean air provides the requisite bacteria that is responsible for fighting off germs that cause diseases. Germs are often the causative agents of various diseases. Fresh air in eradicating this germs, maintains the status core of the body keeping you healthy. The combination of freshwater with clean air incomparable. With this in place, your stress levels will drop subsequently.

Chapter 3. How to Meditate, Relaxation

As you've seen, meditation can be practiced anywhere. Usually, it helps to be alone. However, many larger cities have meditation centers, where you can go and meditate in a room with others. The atmosphere will be quiet and conducive to a peaceful visit.

An open church is an ideal spot, as well, by peaceful methods. Silent mantra meditation works nicely in a quiet, spiritual atmosphere. Christian churches often have stained glass windows, which are ideal for visual methods. The colors and picture will slowly draw you in, leaving your thoughtful comments behind.

Many meditators try to spend two short periods each day in meditation. Twenty minutes in the morning and another twenty later in the day works well to keep you calm and refreshed mentally. If you can only meditate once each day, try to add a bit longer to your practice.

To avoid being disturbed, find a place alone. Turn off your cell phone and put it out of sight so that you won't be worried. If possible, dim the lights. Finally, close the door to keep pets away. Just as they curl up in your lap when you rest or nap, they will sense your calm mind and try to be near you. A happy dog in your lap does not lead to successful meditation.

Advice

Meditation, unlike hypnosis and other states of altered consciousness, has no suspected dangers. You can't get "stuck" in a meditative state, and no one has control over your thoughts or actions. So you have nothing to fear from trying it out. What you have to gain is less tension, lower blood pressure, and control over life's stress.

To begin exploring meditation, try out the methods described here. See which ones fit your life best. See which ones work better and relax you more. The truth is that all of the research into meditation won't affect you. What will make a difference is how the practice makes a difference in your life. To help evaluate, make yourself a little checklist:

- Do I feel relaxed and calm after meditating?
- Are there any unpleasant results? (Groggy, Tired)
- Did any methods seem to work best?
- Did any methods seem not to work as well?
- Will I try meditating again tomorrow?

What does it feel like when you meditate? But as you progress, you may feel a sense of sinking slowly, hearing noises as though you're in a peaceful tunnel. If an alarm or phone rings, you'll be pulled back "up" to full alertness at once. You may feel dizzy if it happens. To avoid this happening too frequently, turn off or silence your cell phone before beginning to meditate. You probably will feel a little dizzy when you "come back" from meditating. You've been losing less oxygen and your pulse is slowed, so give yourself a moment or two to adjust, when you stop.

Honestly, any time you introduce a new habit or practice that will change how you feel, how you react to stress, and how your body responds to tension, it's a a significant change. Life lets us get conditioned. So to change sometimes, we need to do a little re-conditioning. Try the techniques that work best for several days at least. See how you feel in a few days as opposed to after one try. If you feel adventurous, try another technique or combine a couple. The only result can be the improvement. The less we let stress and tension affect us, the healthier and happier we will be.

How To Meditate

Meditation is a great - and logically demonstrated - habit for a solid body and mind. Be that as it may, a few people battle with the time, consistency, center and system required to get meditation right.

What a great many people don't know is, you don't really need to take a seat and close your eyes for a considerable length of time a day - in light of the fact that there are other far less demanding approaches to get your psyche into a thoughtful state, and appreciate the advantages of this ancient practice.

For example:

1. While you walk your dog

As you're strolling Jack, instead of meditating a large number of things you're stalling on, take a stab at giving careful attention to your environment.

Recognize the sounds, the general population, the climate. What do you smell? What would you be able to see? What would you be able to hear out yonder? How does your body feel?

By taking a careful walk, you're discharging endorphins, which enable you to build your joy level, and even diminish stress and live longer.

2. While you make coffee or tea

Begin your morning with more profound concentration, lucidity and peace by rehearsing this simple reflective custom.

As you make your tea or coffee, concentrate your attention on your developments.

Close your eyes and notice the tea, take a taste, enjoy it. Furthermore, as you experience the ritual custom, be deliberately mindful of your breath.

You can likewise apply this while you cook your most loved supper or heat.

3. While you do the dishes

Doing dishes or clearing your floor doesn't need to be an errand. Actually, this is the ideal time for you to associate with yourself and feel grounded.

On the off chance that you see your mind wandering, take yourself back to mindfulness by thinking about the general population and things throughout your life that fill you with delight and appreciation.

4. While you shower

Have you at any point asked why your best thoughts tend to come while you're showering?

"The shower is where we can develop mindfulness. When we get tranquil, when we get still, when we rest, you could state, in mindfulness, our natural drive to see associations that we didn't see the prior minute is unobstructed."

On the off chance that you need to take it somewhat further, as you shower, you can even envision accomplishing your objectives, and the feeling that will wash over you as you do.

5. While you tune in to your main tune

Practicing mindfulness or meditation can be as straightforward as tuning in to your main song - insofar as you're totally centered around your breathing and the feeling that the song brings out in you.

6. While you ride the transport or sit in your auto

Sit serenely. Take long and full breaths. Recognize the warm sun stroking your face. Welcome the delightful city lights or scene. Also, let your mind take you all alone trip.

As you now know, the benefits of meditation can be conveyed into the most ordinary exercises - helping you acknowledge life all the more, inhabit a slower pace, embrace new propensities, and be more joyful.

Practical Advice On Meditation

To what extent Should I Meditate?

In the event that you are new to meditation, I suggest beginning gradually. Begin with only 5 minutes every day. Bit by bit increment the time more than half a month. When I began reflecting, five minutes felt like an unfathomable length of time. I now practice for 30 minutes every day, and here and there I am astonished at how rapidly it passes!

Where Should I Meditate?

Locate a comfortable spot where you can sit. You can sit on the floor (utilizing a pad or pad for help if necessary) or sit upright in a seat, with your feet laying on the floor.

A few people suggest that you don't rests on your back, however I figure you ought to think in whatever stance works for you (unless resting influences you to fall asleep!)

You can meditate anyplace, yet I like having an extraordinary place in my home for my training. You can take in more about making a meditation space in your home here.

What Do I Do?

The least demanding meditation strategy is to count the breath. I forget about each in-breath and breath with a similar number. So my mind concentrates on "One" (in-breath), "One" (out-breath), "Two" (in-breath), "Two" (out-breath), et cetera. When I hit 10 (which seldom occurs before my mind has wandered!) I begin once again at one. On the off chance that you don't care for counting, you can essentially rehash to yourself "in, out.... in, out... "

At the point when your mind wanders, which it WILL DO (that's what the mind does!) tenderly guide your attention back to your breath. On the off chance that you have to begin once again counting in light of the fact that you don't recollect the latest relevant point of interest, that is fine! The key is to not reprimand or judge yourself for giving your attention a chance to wander. Actually ... seeing that your psyche has wandered is the general purpose of meditation you are winding up more mindful of the activities of your mind!

Indeed, even the moderately basic guideline to "take after the breath" can sound somewhat obscure or confounding. A supportive method is to bring your attention where you most notice the vibe of the breath — in the chest and lungs? the nose? the stomach? That is your stay. Each time your mind wanders, return to the physical vibes of relaxing.

At the point when thought emerge, it's anything but difficult to get diverted and tail them and draw in them and explain them and investigate them.... An accommodating practice is to just name the contemplations: "stressing," "arranging," "recollecting." Don't stress over making sense of the exact mark for the kind of thought you're having. Simply "considering" will do, as well!

What's more, if the thoughts don't leave? It's still alright.

I adore that depiction of the training.

How Do I Fit This Into My Day?

The critical thing is to make it a propensity. After numerous long stretches of a reliable practice, it will end up being a vital piece of your day, such as practicing or brushing your teeth!

Changing your habits over some stretch of time really makes new neural systems in your mind, and the training will turn out to be a piece of your day by day schedule.

Knocks along the Road

In Any Case, Nothing's Happening!

Meditation is about non-judgmental mindfulness. We have to not bring desires into our practice. You may encounter a snapshot of significant understanding amid a meditation session. Or, then again you may be truly exhausted. You may feel fretful and disturbed. Or, on the other hand you may feel quiet and relaxed.

Meditation is tied in with grasping whatever is right now. The advantages of meditation — more noteworthy mindfulness and discretion, increased calm and empathy — will rise after some time. In any case, every individual session will be totally unique.

So, in case you're exhausted, simply take note of, "This is the thing that fatigue feels like." If you're content, take note of, "This is the thing that satisfaction feels like."

• Meditating for 10 minutes daily is limitlessly superior to meditating for 70 minutes once per week. Attempt to meditate oftentimes (consistently if conceivable), regardless of the possibility that that just means sitting for a couple of minutes.

• Start little. In the event that you endeavor to meditate for 30 minutes right from the beginning, I can practically ensure that you will get disappointed and disheartened. I prescribe beginning with five minutes, and just increase that time when you're comfortable. Regardless of the possibility that you sit for five minutes, and you find that your mind wanders the entire time, you will in any case get unfathomable advantages from meditation.

• Pick a gentle alarm. On the off chance that your clock is uproarious and jolting, reckoning the caution will occupy your attention amid meditation.

• Meditate in a peaceful place. Having less distractions around you will normally enable you to meditate better, and will make your meditation significantly more profitable.

• Its most straightforward to lose your attention amid your out-breath. You're in-breath is exceptionally articulated and simple to focus on, and the vast majority's mind wanders on their out-breaths (me included). These merits remembering.

• Be simple on yourself when your mind wanders. It's anything but difficult to wind up plainly disappointed with yourself when your mind wanders, yet don't. Your meditations will be substantially more gainful when you delicately bring your mind back.

How Can I Establish A Good Meditation Practice?

One effective way to consistently practice meditation is to create and plan out a practice that you can follow, according to your needs, your daily schedule, routines, and timing.

The thing about meditation is that you need to be mindful of everything that you experience in your session. With mindful meditation, there is a goal and a purpose. It is to help you be conscious and mindful of everything you do.

Benefits Of Establishing A Meditation Practice

A foundation of your meditation session is important because, in many ways, when you set the stones to your practice, your brain will start moving toward making this practice happen. For example, if you decide to buy a new meditation mat, your mind will be reminded (or you will remember) that you purchased the mat, and you want to know the feeling of sitting on the mat and practicing.

Without a firm foundation, you will not be consistent

It won't be long before whatever you're doing eventually crumbles and falls because there's nothing supporting it. That's just one way of describing how important it is to develop a sound meditation practice right from the very beginning of the process.

It helps you create a habit

But although meditation is something that is beneficial for everyone, not everyone is currently putting it into practice. Some people are not practicing meditation at all. Why? Because it isn't a habit. A lot of us lead very busy lives, so sometimes our plates seem too full to take on anything else. There will always be a reason not to start something, which is why it is entirely up to you to make time for it.

The purpose of establishing a meditation practice is because you want to make meditation a habit, a part of your daily life, and something that you are willing to do every day without even thinking twice or resisting it because you are pressed for time.

It makes your practice ingrained, almost second-nature activity in your life

Meditating will become much like how brushing your teeth or showering, preparing something to eat, and even going on a daily commute to work. Those habits are so deeply ingrained in you that you do them without any effort or a lot of thought put into it.

That is what establishing a meditation practice aims to do for you right now, and it is something you need to establish as a foundation to make your practice consistent.

Here is how you can start establishing a meditation practice for yourself.

- Start small. Start small at first by meditating for short periods of time, maybe 5-10 minutes a day, especially if you're new at it. You can do anything for 5-10 minutes a day with no resistance, and the time will pass before you even know it. When you see how easy that was, it keeps you motivated to keep adding onto that. By creating small, achievable goals, you begin building the habit of making meditation a part of your daily life.

- Use tools to help you. There is an app for just about everything these days, even meditation, so why not make the most of the tools you have to help you establish a successful daily practice? There are several apps, such as Headspace and Calm, which can help you enhance your meditation sessions, with everything from timers to ambient sounds to help set the mood. If it helps make your daily practice more enjoyable, why not? You are more likely to stick to something if you like what you're doing.

- Use YouTube. Guided meditations that you like on YouTube can be a great tool, especially for beginners on this journey. It helps you stay on track and on the right path. Some meditations are given on a daily basis, whereas some are based on your goals, such as Meditation for Focus and Meditation for Sleep. Guided meditations make it much easier for beginners, especially to start getting into the flow of things and helps you progress in the right direction with your meditation sessions, especially when you're doing it alone as a solo practice. It would be good to know that you are heading in the right direction.

- Make space. This is extremely important. Making space in your home or anywhere you feel comfortable is a vital part of your practice. A space that is dedicated solely for your meditation sessions should be a place that is safe and comfortable for you, and preferably quiet. Fill that space with anything you need to make you feel comfortable or something that makes you feel like you want to be there for a while. You can fill it with pillows, cushions, pictures that inspire you, incense or scented candles if it helps, and anything that helps soothe your soul and brings you a sense of calm. That will go a long way toward helping you make meditation a consistency in your life if you have a space that you look forward to spending some time in each day because of the comfort and calm that it envelopes you in.

- Make it a schedule. Okay, so not many people like routine and schedule, but if you are starting in meditation practices, this is essential. Make it a point to pencil it into your calendar or make a note of it on your calendar app on your phone. It can be easy for other things going on during the day to take precedence over your meditation session, which is why you need to purposely make that time just to stop and meditate before the day comes to an end, and you realize you didn't get to spend any time meditating at all.

When Is A Good Time To Meditate?

The short answer to this is preferably at a quiet time and as long as this time works for you. You can choose to meditate in the morning, afternoon, evening, or even before you go to bed. That's the beauty of this practice; it is entirely up to what works best for you. Every individual is different, and no two people are going to be doing things the exact same way with the same experience. Some people prefer to meditate in the morning because it sets the tone for the rest of the day, while some prefer to do it at night because it helps them unwind, calm down, and relax after a long and hectic day.

The best time of the day for you to meditate would be any time that you can consistently and realistically commit to it. It can be in the morning, in the afternoon, in the evening, or at night; it doesn't matter. As long as you are getting it done, that is the only thing that matters, even if it is for just 10 minutes a day. A short meditation session is better than nothing at all.

When I'm meditating, is there a specific posture I need to follow?

No, there isn't because again, everyone is different, and some people may prefer one posture, while someone else may prefer another. That is okay. The posture you decide to go with should be the one that feels most comfortable and what you are happy with. If sitting in a chair works better for you, go ahead and do that. If you prefer to sit cross-legged on a mat, that's alright. If you prefer to lie down, that's alright too. It is important to do what is right for your body and what you feel most connected with, which will allow you to relax yet stay alert during your session at the same time.

Making Use of Meditation Anchors

Even the most advanced meditation practitioners could use an anchor every now and then. Our minds are such a versatile thing that sometimes it can get easily distracted and wander before we become aware and bring it back to focus again. This is why meditation anchors are helpful, especially if you are new to this practice. It will help you find the focus and concentration that you need during your meditation session. Even if you're an advanced practitioner, having an anchor is still going to be helpful to you on the days when your mind may be struggling to grasp the concentration that it needs.

A meditation anchor will allow you to steady your mind and maintain focus on what you are doing. An anchor gives you a point to bring your mind back to whenever it deigns to wander of. An anchor gives you something to connect your mind as you strengthen and build on mindfulness, a practice that will eventually come with time.

A meditation anchor can be anything that you find useful and which helps you to maintain your focus. Some suggestions of what could be used as an anchor when you meditate include the following:

- Focusing on your breath as it moves in and out of your body
- What your body feels like with each deep breath you take
- Your chest as it rises and falls slowly and rhythmically with each breath that moves in and out
- If you're using music or any ambient tones to help set the mood, you can focus on that and the way it makes you feel as you listen to the rhythm
- Physical sensations that slowly emerge as you progress throughout the meditation, for example, the way your hands feel or the way the muscles in your body feel

Are you starting to get the idea? Your anchor can be anything that you want it to be. It doesn't have to be specific to the list. It just has to be something that you can connect on, something that your mind can focus on while you meditate. It helps you give you a purpose, especially when you're just starting out. Otherwise, you could find yourself aimlessly sitting on the mat, wondering if you're doing it right or not being able to meditate at all.

This would be a good time to find an anchor that works best for you and helps you with your meditation practice. Being able to bring your thoughts back to your anchor when needed will be a great help in your four-week plan to achieve a deeper state of meditation.

Having a regular anchor that is consistent would be helpful, but if you ever feel that you want to choose or use something else as your anchor, go ahead and do it. If it helps you stay focused, and it works for you, your anchor can be anything you want it to be. Remember, it is all about finding what works best for you because meditation is such a personal experience, one that is entirely yours.

How to Reduce Stress By Meditating?

So what is stress? Stress is the body's way of responding to pressure that may be exerted on it physically or psychologically. Stress is caused when the body releases stress chemicals, usually adrenaline, into the blood to combat whatever pressure it is confronted with. Stress can be classified as follows:

- Survival stress. This is stress that we face when we are confronted by dangerous situations where you feel that physical harm is imminent. It is here where we have a fight-and-flight response to fight stress.

- Internal stress. This is stress caused by worries over things that are out of your control. Simply put, internal stress is self-imposed stress that can be avoided by not giving yourself so much pressure over things that are beyond you.

- Environmental stress. This is stress caused by factors in your surroundings, like noise. Stay away from environmental stress triggers, and you will have a happy life.

- Tiredness. This type of stress is caused by fatigue, which usually accumulates over a long period due to such things as overworking.

Stress is an inescapable part of life, and sooner or later, we experience it. What we need to do is learn how to manage it so that it does not overwhelm us and take over our lives. Stress is not an entirely bad thing as it can enhance our alertness and concentration. However, in excess, it is very unhealthy.

Symptoms of Stress

How do you know if you are stressed? The following are some signs that will let you know if you are stressed.

Cognitive symptoms:

- Problems remembering things
- Low concentration
- High anxiety
- Constant worry

- Emotional symptoms:
- Being moody
- Highly irritable and angry
- Loneliness and reclusion
- Sadness

Physical symptoms:

- Low libido
- Aches and pain
- High heart rate
- Dizziness

Behavioral symptoms:

- Eating disorders (bingeing or self-starving)
- Lack of sleep
- Substance abuse
- Nervousness

Causes of Stress

External causes:

- Major life changes (divorce, chronic illness, the death of a loved one)
- Work burden
- Financial problems
- Trauma

Internal causes:

- Constant worry
- Negativity and pessimism
- Fear and anxiety
- Unrealistic expectations

Side Effects of Stress

Stress can cause serious health and social problems if it is not dealt with immediately and well. Here are some of the side effects of stress:

- Mental disorders, like depression and anxiety
- Weight problems, such as obesity
- Problems with menstrual cycles
- Skin and hair problems (acne, hair loss, etc.)
- Sexual dysfunction
- Gastrointestinal problems, like ulcerative colitis

Meditation and Stress Management

Meditation has been proven as a stress reliever and is being embraced by many for relaxation. Stress relief needs both mental and physical relaxation, and meditation provides that. To understand why meditation is so helpful in reducing stress, we should know what it takes to relax:

Deep breathing. Deep breathing is a quick and sure way of deflating stress from your system. This is a simple technique with far-reaching positive consequences in keeping stress in check.

Balancing the nervous system. For the body to function optimally, the nervous system must be at equilibrium. You must be at peace mentally. Stress destabilizes this balance, and the only way to stead your system is by relaxation. A state of profound serenity of the nervous system is the counter to stress.

Yoga: Yoga is a series of steady movement and stationary poses combined with deep breathing. Yoga reduces stress and improves flexibility, strength, balance, and stamina if practiced regularly. Almost all types of yoga are beneficial for stress and anxiety relief as they combine steady movement, deep breathing, and stretching. You may try the following types:

Satyananda. This is a traditional form of yoga that uses meditation, gentle poses, and deep relaxation and is ideal for those who want to start practicing for stress and anxiety relief.

Hatha Yoga. This is also a gentle form that is ideal for you to ease your way into practice.

Power Yoga. Power yoga is more advanced and is for those who are already familiar with the basics. It is more intense, and the focus is on fitness. This is ideal for those seeking relaxation and stimulation.

Tai Chi. Tai Chi is a mellow form of meditation suited for everyone. It is especially good for the elderly recovering from injuries and illnesses common with those of advanced age. It is a series of slow body movements, emphasizing concentration, circulation of energy through the body, and relaxation while focusing on breathing.

For you to effectively deal with stress and anxiety through meditation, it is important to be consistent in practicing whichever type of meditation you settle for. Make it part of your life. Practice it regularly until it becomes second nature. Here is what you need to do for a successful stress-relieving meditation experience:

Get a quiet, serene place for your meditation exercise; this can be anywhere as long as it has no interference. It can be in your backyard, living room, in a park, etc.

Assume a comfortable posture, whether seated, standing, or lying down. Start tuning your mind to the here and now. Focus and concentrate.

In the posture with eyes closed, take a slow deep breath and relax your body as you do this. Get into an inhaling and exhaling rhythm.

Clear your mind of distracting thoughts and concentrate on your meditation. Pay attention to your breathing, and concentrate on that only as you relax.

Channel your mind to happy thoughts of a happy place you have been, or just concentrate on the present while listening to your breathing. Push out unwanted thoughts that may come your way.

Keep your eyes closed, take deep breaths, and imagine your body relaxing. Keep doing this until you are completely relaxed.

Imagine a life of reduced anxiety and stress. Isn't that what we all want? By following the advice and tips discussed above, you will be able to effectively kick out stress from your life and remain a happy and relaxed individual. Whenever stress is left to get out of control, depression sets in. Depression is a condition that is directly linked to the mismanagement of stress. Depression is an extreme form of stress. Let us understand what depression is and how meditation can help in its relief.

Fighting Depression Through Meditation

In this section, we shall look at how meditation can be adopted in the management and cure of depression and why it is gaining acceptance as an alternative to clinical medicine in the treatment and management of this condition. Depression is a disorder of a person's mood or emotions, causing sadness and loss of interest.

When one is faced with extreme emotions or feelings of hopelessness, anxiety, sadness, despair, or low self-esteem, they can be considered depressed. This type of depression is situational as it is triggered by circumstances that the person is dealing with. Clinically, depression is caused by a chemical imbalance in the brain, causing bipolar disorder and manic depression, which are generally referred to as an organic depression. Stress hormones (cortisol and epinephrine) found in adrenaline has been proven responsible for organic depression.

Depression is usually exhibited or accompanied by the following symptoms:

- Loss of interest in hobbies and usual activities
- Reclusiveness
- Feelings of hopelessness and worthlessness
- Difficulty or lack of sleep
- Restlessness and fatigue
- Lower concentration
- Suicidal thoughts

Once in a while, we all face some form of mild depression. Unfortunately, some of us experience extreme forms of this condition that can overwhelm them leading to significant mental deterioration, social self-exclusion, and even suicides.

Causes of Depression

Depression is caused by several factors or, in some instances, a combination of these factors. They are as follows:

- A chronic and long illness
- Some personality traits are more vulnerable to depression (e.g. low self-esteem)
- Family history (those from families where some have suffered depression before are highly likely to be affected)
- Giving birth (some women get postnatal depression because of physical and emotional changes)

- Loneliness and drug abuse
- Chemical changes in the brain (clinical depression)
- Physical and emotional abuse
- Some medicines
- Conflicts

The good news is that depression can significantly be managed and even treated through meditation, as we shall learn herein.

Anger Management

Anger describes an unpleasant emotion characterized by strong feelings of antagonism and displeasure that ranges from mild irritability or annoyance to intense fury or rage. Our triggers for anger differ from person to person, however, we are exposed to these triggers often. Anger is a normal human emotion that when recognized and appropriate action is taken to deal with it can bear positive outcomes. In this case, it may even become a motivator inspiring one to advocate for social change or stand up for certain injustices. Anger notifies us when we need to take action and rectify something while giving us the motivation, strength, and energy to act. However, when anger is unresolved or left unchecked it can lead to inappropriate and/or aggressive behavior. In this case, it may be referred to as a 'negative' emotion.

Over the past few years especially in the industrial and the now post-industrial era, there has been a significant and continuous rise in stress and anger. This shows that stress has a role in influencing anger. If one is more prone to anger then a lot of stress is likely to trigger feelings of anger. When stress becomes too much and ceases to be a motivator, it may cause us to feel irritable or just angry to the core. When this happens, one is usually overwhelmed with tons of stressors and typically one feels like they lack the resources to deal with stress effectively and has an outburst of anger. This type of stress is referred to as distress. If stressors are understood and steps are taken to maintain equilibrium and deal with the stress, then one can limit distress thereby controlling and limiting one's anger.

Techniques for Anger Relaxation and Management

Techniques for anger relaxation are frequently used in anger management therapy to help us understand our anger and act in ways that are positive to alleviate the negative aspects of anger rather than suppress feelings of anger. These techniques work most effectively when practiced frequently. Some of the techniques are as follows:

Controlled Deep Breathing

When we get angry, several subtle physical changes occur and notify us of these feelings. One of the most noticeable is the change in breathing. When one is angry or upset, their breathing becomes shallow and quick. Noticing this is one of the first steps of this technique. Once one noticed the change in breath, one can make a deliberate effort to deepen and slow their breathing –this will help in maintaining control. These breaths ought to come from your belly rather than your chest. The breaths should be twice as long when coming out as when coming in, for instance, one may breathe in slowly as they count to four and breathe out even slower as they count to eight.

This slow, deep, and deliberate breathing will help relax your breath and return into a normal, relaxed state. Since all things present in the body are interconnected, controlling, and relaxing one's breath should in turn control and relax muscle tensions that are caused by anger thereby reducing feelings of anger significantly.

Progressive Muscle Relaxation

One of the other noticeable physical changes related to anger is muscle tension. This tension can manifest in different parts of one's body and can collectively clump in specific areas such as the neck and shoulders. This tension can even remain long after the anger is gone. Progressive muscle relaxation involves deliberately tensing and tightening your muscles both stressed and unstressed for a slow count of ten then relaxing or releasing these tightened muscles. When practicing this, be sure to release muscles immediately you feel pain. This technique requires you to work progressively from one muscle group to another (for example from head to toe) until you have taken each muscle through a cycle of tension and release. With diligent practice, one may notice their ability to do this cycle of the full body in a few minutes. This technique of tightening and releasing muscles can prove more relaxing than relaxation itself.

Visualizing Yourself to Calmness

Visualization refers to the mental formation or representation of an object, image, situation or set of information. Visualization techniques can also be employed to help with the management of anger. Our brains constantly visualize in the process of simulating future scenarios. This visualization happens so effortlessly that we barely notice it in the same way we barely notice our breathing. When we become aware of our visualization, we can use it as a tool to reduce or reverse anger. Visualization to help with anger is done by imagining a place or scenario that makes you feel calm or relaxed and focusing on details (sometimes with the aid of audio material such as music) such as smells, sounds and how good it feels to be in that space. This is usually done when one is sited comfortably and quietly with their eyes closed.

Visualization has four key benefits that improve how we deal with anger. Firstly, it rewires and programs one's brain to help them realize the strategies, tools, and resources they can use to achieve peace and harmony away from anger. Secondly, it builds our intrinsic motivation to take actions necessary to change the habit pattern of the mind, which is reacting to anger. Thirdly, it sparks one's creative subconscious, which helps us with the sublimation of these negative feelings into more socially acceptable forms of expression such as dance, poetry, music among others. This sublimation helps us express rather than suppress these feelings of anger. Lastly, visualization aids in the law of attraction thereby drawing you closer to circumstances, resources, tools, and people who can help you achieve your goals of anger management.

Various meditation techniques are also used in anger management and relaxation. Mindfulness meditation and Vipassana meditation both encourage us to accept the anger when it manifests itself and observe it as it is without reacting to it or engaging with it. This usually causes us to be fueled and consumed by it causing it to become problematic. In retrospect, when we just simply observe anger as an emotion, neither good nor bad, we learn to work with anger, as it is however or whenever it arises skillfully without it spiraling out of control. When we engage in guided meditation we learn how to relax and gain relief from stress and stressors that may end up causing anger and allow us to process these feelings healthily. This technique can be used with children too especially those with heavy temper tantrums. Peaceful and guided meditations help children, adults, and teens improve self-esteem, relieve anxiety, and stress, and feel generally refreshed in mind, body, and spirit and develop positive mental attitudes in their daily activities.

Chapter 4. The Best Kind of Meditation Done for You

Be in the moment. Be in the light of the candle or in the presence of the photo and breathe as you breathe for meditation. Breathe in through the nostrils to the count of eight and out to the count of ten. Keep breathing in this manner until the breathing rhythm becomes comfortable. Now place your eyes on the object that you have chosen and do not look away. It doesn't matter if you blink. It doesn't matter if thoughts come to your mind, but if they do, banish them until a later time and go back to thinking about the breathing. Look at the photo if you are using a photograph and notice every element of the photo without creating a chain of thought in your mind. Look at the candle flame – if you are using a candle – and notice how it changes with each moment that passes. The flicker of the flame can be very inspirational.

Meditation of this kind can last up to 20 minutes, and then you need to wait for a moment before you get up, so that your heartbeat and blood pressure can go back to normal. Say a little prayer of thanks for the moment of meditation and finish off by writing what you feel in your journal. Although this may have very little significance at the time of writing your journal, you will be able to go back to it at a later stage and use it to recall how you felt and whether this system of meditation worked for you or what you need to do to make it work better. For example, if you didn't pull the drapes too, then perhaps this will help you to concentrate better next time. Perhaps the photograph brought about memories. Don't get too self-indulgent, but simply note down the emotions. This isn't about reliving something. It's about living with it in the now, and the flicker of the candle flame helps you to appreciate that every moment brings change into your life. The meditation helps you to find inner peace at a time when your thoughts are taking over and gives you respite so that you can comfortably face whatever it is that you are going through.

You can do this kind of meditation in conjunction with your normal daily meditation. For example, perform your normal meditation in the morning and try guided meditation later in the day when thoughts have had a chance to penetrate into your consciousness and make you feel negative about life. This will help you to feel more able to cope with whatever it is that you have had to go through. If you feel that it will help you, then doing a guided meditation with the help of a meditation teacher will be a wise move as this will help you to gain the right posture and do things in the right order among others or simply on a one to one basis with your teacher.

This is also a kind of meditation that you can do when you are inspired by things around you. For example, there's nothing wrong with being inspired by a natural environment, and you can simply sit and breathe and observe that natural environment during the day and at the same time, build your inner strength.

When the mind is filled with thoughts, it is nicknamed the "monkey mind" and these quiet moments of calm can help to tame the monkey mind so that the only thoughts that are in your mind at any time are those relevant to that moment in time. That's extremely useful for stressful times of your life and is not avoidance. It is merely an acknowledgment that your mind needs to be clear so that you can perform those tasks ahead of you with clarity. A calm mind is the best gift that you can give to yourself, and awareness of your thoughts helps you to program your mind to be able to recognize the beauty of the world that you live in and what it has to offer you at that particular moment you meditate. When you finish the meditation, you will find that the clarity continues, and your thought patterns change so that you are able to put them into order and see things in a much clearer way.

Mindfulness Meditation In Your Life In General

Quite often, during the course of a lifetime, you find times when you have sufficient time to meditate, but when you may not have the required stillness of mind. The stillness of mind is what meditation helps you with, and the reason that you are finding it difficult is because of all of the negativity of life or the fact that you are overwhelmed with thoughts.

Think of your thoughts like cardboard boxes. Each of them takes up space in your mind, and you can do the following exercise to try and eliminate some of those boxes so that you are able to think clearly and positively about your life in general. These exercises will help you to encourage mindfulness into your life and are useful at times of stress so that you can go back to a position where you are able to concentrate once again getting rid of the feeling of being bogged down by thoughts that you really don't want in your mind, but that keep persisting. They are quite simple exercises to perform and will help you to use mindfulness to bring you back into a state of non-judgment and neutrality when the world you live in pushes you a little too far for your comfort.

Using the raisin exercise

This exercise is easy for you to perform at any time during your day. The texture of a raisin is absolutely perfect, and as this is something you can easily carry with you, it's an exercise you can do at any time of day when you find that thoughts are overloading your mind. Take the raisin from its packet and hold it in your hand. Banish all other thoughts. Look at the shape of the raisin, the wrinkles that it has and the size of the raisin and then pop it into your mouth, concentrating on the taste of the raisin and the texture as you chew it sufficiently to swallow it. Although eating a raisin takes only a couple of minutes, it can help you to get back to a state of mindfulness when you know that life is throwing you lemons, and you want time to respond. This will calm you and help you to get back to a state of neutrality, which is useful in your everyday dealings with people.

The good thing about this exercise is that you instantly take away your concentration on problems by examining the raisin before you place it in your mouth. Press it with your fingers and watch how it changes shape. As the mind is only able to think about one thing at a time, you take the edge off your normal thoughts and give them less credence. It is not a case of avoidance, but you are able to digest your problem when you are calmer and come up with better solutions than you would by addressing it with a mind filled with mixed thoughts.

An exercise in observation

This is useful for those who work in busy offices, but who are able to escape to the park at lunchtime. Find a place to sit where you are in a peaceful environment. The idea is to observe what is happening around you while deep breathing, but instead of putting labels on things, merely observe the colors and the textures and the sights and the sounds without having to call things by their names. Instead of doing that, simply enjoy the movement of the leaves in the trees, the formation of clouds in the sky, or the sound of laughter, without having to label it and judge it. The moment that you judge something as good or bad, you are stepping away from mindfulness. You should be mindful that you are surrounded with so much abundance, but not label it at all. Simply focus on the colors and the smells, the textures, and the mélange of things that touch your senses.

This will help you with your meditation because this kind of numbness is what you are trying to achieve when you meditate.

It's like putting your mind into neutral gear and going along for the ride. You don't have to judge anything. You don't see women who are overly large as being fat. You don't judge kids that are noisy as being anything other than kids. You simply BE in the moment and let the world pass you by almost in the abstract while enjoying the senses that the world offers you within that moment. It's a useful exercise in that it takes away all of the boxes of thoughts that you have stacked in your mind and allows you a moment of creativity where you don't actually try to create anything, but the world around you creates it for you, like a kaleidoscope of colors and sounds, aromas and atmospheres. This moment is the only one that matters. It is now.

The Buddhist Exercise

Just as the Buddhists believe that your actions form part of who you are, they also believe that there is a path that takes you to where you are, and that will lead you forward in your life, and this is called the Four Noble Truths. You don't have to be Buddhist to understand that they are common sense and can help you to accept your suffering in life as part of who you are. Let's look at the Four Noble Truths so that you can see how they relate to anyone even if you are not Buddhist in your beliefs or philosophy:

- Pain exists
- Pain has a cause
- Pain comes to an end

- You will find a way to end suffering

It's pretty easy to understand, isn't it? Say you cut your finger. It hurts, so pain exists. It has a cause – you must have caught your finger on something, and with sleep and recuperation, in a week's time, the pain won't be there anymore. Thus, you have found a way to end that suffering. It's very basic at this level and gets more complex when you deal with emotional problems and how to solve them.

- Pain exists – I feel bad
- Pain has a cause – I have reasons that justify feeling bad
- Pain comes to an end – Acceptance of pain will help to end it
- Finding a way to end the suffering – often, this comes in the form of self-care.

So, we can use the Buddhist philosophy to take a look at our hurt or our feelings in life and start to examine why we feel that way. The first answer lies in caring for yourself, so placing your hand upon your heart, you can tell yourself that you know that suffering exists. Then you can accept that suffering is a human reaction, so be comfortable with it as being a normal response to stimuli. Give yourself a hug and let yourself feel that you are acknowledging those feelings. Then mindfully breathe for a moment and accept that you are entitled to the feelings and that they don't make you less of a person. At this stage, simply repeat an affirmation such as this or make your own affirmation to help you to get beyond the pain that you are suffering:

"I love and accept myself regardless of the way that I am feeling and know that these feelings are simply a part of the perfect person that I am."

Often the reason for the fight in mind between different thoughts is because we don't feel entitled to feel pain. We argue with our reasons and fill our minds up with all kinds of justifications and self-doubt and often blame ourselves for being negative. Well, it's okay to be negative. It's okay to be positive. It's okay to be you and to accept each moment as it presents itself without adding the complexity of thoughts that make us feel bad about ourselves. Self-acceptance and love were part of the Maslow equation, and it wouldn't hurt for you to make a copy of that equation and remind yourself occasionally that you have needs that must be met as well as trying your hardest to meet the needs of others. Accept that this moment will pass because there is no doubt that it will, and start to breathe for relief of those problems. Breathe in, and be happy to be. Breathe out and feel happy to dispel thoughts that burden you. Breathe in and feel the fresh air entering your lungs. When you are emotional, your breathing becomes erratic, and this exercise helps you to feel that your feelings are justified and that you are able to deal with problems without breaking yourself down into a million pieces. This moment will pass when you accept that the Buddhist philosophy works. Problems come and go in your life and are a part of who you are. Accept your imperfections and embrace them because they make you into a unique human being.

A mindfulness exercise using touch

This is a fun exercise that you can share with your kids or with friends. The idea is that they place many different objects with different textures into containers where you cannot see what you are about to touch. While you breathe deeply and close your eyes, your hand is guided to the box, and you must try to use your senses to distinguish what it is that you are touching. From the grains of rice to the complex patterns of pasta, there are so many different textures that you will experience at the touch of a hand, and this helps you to restore your sense of touch and to recognize the beauty that touches places into your life.

A mindfulness exercise using taste

It is advised that you do this exercise with other students of mindfulness who will be aware of the need to recognize different tastes. You should also let them know of dislikes or dietary differences you may have. Placed in bowls, different food substances are tested randomly, and the idea is to be mindful as you taste each one of them. It's quite surprising to note that the 21st-century diet has changed the way that we taste things. If you use natural elements such as fruit yogurt, different fruits, nuts, and elements that are varied in taste and texture, you take the food onto your tongue and do not swallow until you have investigated using your taste buds to distinguish what it is that you are eating. Slow everything down and discover the world of taste.

A mindfulness exercise using color

Many of us take for granted the colors that surround our lives, and at this very moment, you will be surrounded by color. If you take an object of color and concentrate on it while you breathe in and out as you do with meditation, notice the different hues of that color and try not to be distracted to other colors surrounding that color. Then feast your eyes on something that has many colors and try to distinguish which color is the most predominant while you breathe and simply be, rather than going through all the thoughts or preconceptions you have about color. See the colors, rather than the objects. See the beauty, rather than the likes and dislikes. See the intensity rather than the shade and how you can improve it. It's a great little exercise in breathing and one that you can do at any time without anyone knowing what you are doing. It helps you to appreciate the world around you through the sense of sight.

Mindfulness exercise with hearing

For this exercise, I want you to sit in a natural environment away from the road and away from the hustle-bustle of life and sit in your meditation position. Breathe in and breathe out as you have been taught, but in this instance, the only relevant part of your body is your ears and what you hear. It could be a songbird. It may be a distant rustle of the leaves. It may be silence, but the idea is that you let the ears take your thoughts away from the world in general and into the realm of listening. You may be surprised at the noises of the world, the silence that comes with the morning mist, or the majesty that you feel in the presence of a thunderstorm. We do not use our senses sufficiently at this moment in time, and this is a great exercise to open up your connection with the world around you and enjoy all that it offers.

I don't expect you to remember all of these exercises, so it's handy to carry the book with you and to use it when you feel that you have a few moments that you would like to fill with mindfulness. You will be surprised that very soon you will notice things in the world around you even when you are not expecting to simply because you have become mindful in the way that you approach your life in general and these moments are very precious ones that will remind you of why you started your mindfulness meditation journey.

You may even find that your tastes change. We are very influenced by what surrounds us, but when you experiment with new foods, new music, new sounds, etc., you get to know your true feelings about the world around you that is influenced by nothing except your own perception. It's all part of getting to know yourself better and using your body to help to communicate with your mind more frequently instead of always being influenced by the world around you and social judgments. You will also experience peace with certain exercises and can use this experience to help you to surround your life with those colors, textures, tastes, and even sounds that fill your heart with happiness.

Chapter 5. How to Set Your Mind to Make Meditation a Habit

Relaxation Techniques

Relaxation is a state of mental and physical calmness and serenity, where one is free from tension and anxiety. A response christened "relaxation response" is elicited when one is relaxed. It is the opposite of stress response experienced when one is under pressure. Meditation is one sure way of generating the relaxation response.

Regular meditation will regularly generate a relaxation response, giving you more control of your body for a stress-free life. The following are the most used relaxation techniques:

Progressive muscle relaxation. This technique is used for relaxing deep muscle tension. Tension in the muscles increases anxiety, and this technique will reduce muscle tension and lower the heart rate and blood pressure. It can be practiced while lying on your back or seated. You tense each muscle group for a few seconds and relax. This is repeated until the whole body relaxes.

Tense/Relax method. This technique is similar to progressive relaxation where you tense and relax muscles for relaxation.

Autogenic method. This method is also about muscle control to make one calmer and relaxed.

Guided imagery or visualization method. This can be used in conjunction with progressive relaxation or by itself. After you have relaxed your muscles, you can get into the visualization method, and use mental imagery to relax your mind. Visualization method is a variation on traditional forms of meditation techniques that require that you use all senses—vision, taste, feel/touch, hearing, and smell. Visualization method entails the creation of an image in your mind that leaves you feeling at peace and free to release all tension and anxiety.

Self-hypnosis. Once you reach a state of deep relaxation as possible, you are more open to suggestions, allowing the hypnotherapist to target and improve a particular aspect of thought.

Deep breathing. Deep breathing emphasizes breathing control and focusing on your breathing to achieve a relaxed state. Take deep breaths from the stomach breathing in enough air into your lungs. Deep breaths mean more oxygen into your system. More oxygen means less tension and anxiety. Deep breathing is simple, but it is a powerful relaxation technique that is easily learned by all and can be done almost anywhere. It offers a quick fix for managing stress levels.

Remember that deep breathing is the basis of other relaxation techniques, and it can be applied together with other relaxation tools like aromatherapy and music. You can use the following routine for your deep breathing meditative technique:

- Sit with your back straight. Place a hand on your chest and the other hand on your stomach. The hands should guide you through the breathing routine.

- Breathe in using your nose. The hand placed on your tummy will be pushed up while the other on your chest will move very little.

- Breathe out from your mouth, releasing the most air you can manage while constricting your stomach muscles. The hand placed on your stomach will move inward as you breathe out while the hand on your chest will hardly move.

- Continue breathing in using your nose and exhaling through your mouth. Breathe in sufficient air so that your lower tummy rises and drops.

- Count down slowly as you breathe out.

- If breathing from your abdomen is a problem while you are seated, lie on a flat surface. The floor is ideal.

- Place a visible light object on your tummy to act as a guide and then breathe so that the object rises as you breathe in and falls as you breathe out.

Every time you want to embark on a relaxation technique, do the following:

- Find a quiet spot where you will not be disturbed.

- Get into a comfortable position, can be sitting or lying down.

- Loosen your clothes and free your arms and legs.

- Dim your lights.

Mastering these relaxation techniques will take time. Over time, your body will be in tune with the sequence of the relaxation techniques. With this mastery, you will be able to get deeper relaxation. Make these practices part of your lifestyle and do them daily. As much as it may be difficult to find exclusive time for meditation, these techniques can be put into practice as you engage in doing other things.

You can meditate on a bus or while commuting for concentrative meditation. Mindfulness techniques can be put into play while walking or exercising your pet or while taking a lunch break at the park. Nonetheless, if you can designate a daily time for relaxation, do so for predictability and ease. Do not try these relaxation techniques while sleepy as you will fall asleep and miss out on your target for relaxation. Relaxation requires maximum concentration and alertness.

No one is perfect, especially at the beginning. Do not pinch yourself for missing some sessions. The main goal is to build momentum so that after a while, you can get into a rhythm and routine.

Peace of Mind

Peace of mind is the key to true life. Happiness, good health, and success are things that should be accessed by every one of us. Meditation is one of the ways that you can do to attain the mental peace that will give you a wholesome life. When we look at the many benefits of meditative practices listed earlier, they refer to or are a testament to a state where one's body is in total control and fully functional.

Bad habits are jettisoned for purer, health-conscious ones. Mental strength and brain functioning are greatly improved and nurtured. Immunity is boosted, leading to fewer or no diseases affecting us. We are less stressed and a lot happier when we meditate regularly. This happiness and well-being are what spawn peace of mind. One becomes aware and in tune with themselves. Full self-awareness is achieved, and with that comes the peace. When your mind is peaceful, you will be more productive. You will relate better with people around you. Your family, friends, colleagues, and strangers that you bump into will notice the difference in how you relate. You become more likable as the happiness and peace you exude rubs off onto others.

Meditation, indeed, leads to peace of mind. Take up meditation, won't you?

Quick and Simple Techniques for A Beginner's Practice

Now that you have all the basic knowledge you need, it is time to delve into the practice itself. There are many kinds of meditation techniques that you can get acquainted with.

Fast and Simple: Techniques on The Go

There are just too many people out there who do not have enough time in their hands but still want to practice meditation. Although meditation can be done anywhere and in almost any circumstance, you must start with some beginner-friendly practices that will not take up too much time. All the exercises in this section can be done within ten minutes, but you can make it last longer if you want.

When you are using certain techniques to fit a certain time frame, you have to put all thought of time constraints out of your head. It would be best if you chose a short time after you wake up or just before you go to bed. Keep in mind that making your mind be still is not easily accomplished, especially for a beginner. But also know that this can become simpler and easier as you go along, so don't let yourself be discouraged by any short-term setbacks.

Basic Meditation with Affirmation

This basic meditation technique is a great way to start your practice. This starts with the basics, and you can add visualizations or added stillness later on.

Sit on the floor or a chair, and keep your back as straight as possible without straining yourself. Make sure that you are comfortable and can hold the position for at least five minutes. Choose a place where you won't be disturbed.

Breathe deeply and relax your body as you breathe. As this is probably your first time, it might be wise to keep your eyes closed throughout the process.

Choose a phrase that you would like to affirm in your life. Try to use the first person, and make sure it is something meaningful to you. Examples can include the following: "There is peace inside me," "I am worthy of love," or "God watches over me."

Take slow, measured breaths. Make your breathing as easy and relaxed as possible, and empty your mind of other thoughts.

Now, repeat the affirmation to yourself quietly. Try to focus only on the affirmation. If you do get distracted by random thoughts, allow the thought to pass rather than suppress it. Simply return your attention to the affirmation gently.

If you find it difficult to focus on a purely mental effort, you can try to whisper the words to yourself, moving your tongue without really speaking a word. Join your breathing with your affirmation and repeat the phrase as you breathe out.

Continue this exercise for at least five minutes. Remember not to get frustrated as your body will end up tensing rather than relaxing. Notice how you felt during the exercise. Was focusing your attention on affirmations and breathing difficult for you? What kinds of thoughts did you find popping into your head?

Focused Breathing

When you can manage to stay focused on affirmations, it is time you focus solely on the breath. This is a great way to develop focused awareness, concentration, and stillness of the mind. Do not expect to have a quiet mind right away. This is all normal and will improve as you continue your practice.

Sit comfortably with your back straight in a place where you will not be disturbed.

Breathe deeply and relax your body. You can choose to close your eyes or keep them open. However, if you find that your thoughts still tend to race around you, keeping your eyes closed will help keep distractions at the minimal.

Turn your attention toward the sensation of your breath. This is a good time to practice the beginner's mind. Experience your breathing as if for the first time. Feel your chest rise and fall as you breathe. Listen intently to the sound of each breath, and feel the air enter and leave your body.

Continue this meditation for at least five minutes. Since you are focusing solely on your breathing, you might find yourself easily distracted by random thoughts and emotions. Do not be alarmed or critical of yourself when this happens. Simply acknowledge the thought or emotion without judgment, and then let it go. Gently direct your focus back to your breathing.

It would be beneficial for you to continue practicing these techniques before you move on to more complex practices. As the basic core of almost all the meditation practices involves awareness of the breath and concentration, these techniques are great if you simply want to stay with the basics or if you want to move on and deepen your practice.

Rolling Up Your Sleeves: Longer and Deeper Practices

You can liken your mind to a deep lake. If you only look at the surface (the ordinary mind), you are often blind to the wonders underneath. When you start practicing focused awareness, you are learning to swim in the waters of your mind. Once you start getting better at swimming, then you can start diving deeper into the depths. This section will introduce more intermediate practices that allow you to get a good look into your psyche. The exercises in this section should be done for twenty minutes or more. You can extend the length of your practice according to your preference and needs.

Body-Tuning Technique

This technique is one of the most important intermediate techniques in meditation as it gets you back in touch with your body. A great majority of people in society are fragmented. The mind is often torn in fragments of positive and negative emotions that aren't fully explored. Worst of all, the body is disconnected from awareness and the mind. This technique aims to get the mind and body reconnected to make them whole again.

This meditation must be done lying down. Find a flat, solid surface that allows for comfort but not so much that you can end up drifting off to sleep.

Direct your awareness of your body as a whole. Pay attention to every sensation that you feel. Feel the places where your body touches the surface of where you're lying on. Feel the cool breeze that wafts through the room or the warmth of your own body.

After a few minutes of full-body awareness, gently direct your attention toward the biggest toe of your left foot.

Start visualizing your breath flow in and out of your toe, bringing the much-needed energy with it. When you're ready, expand your awareness toward your whole left foot and continue to breathe in and out of it. Continue this for at least two minutes.

Once you are done, let your awareness travel upward to your ankles and lower leg. Be patient with yourself, and continue visualizing your breath going in and out in waves across this area of your body.

From here, go up to your knees and thighs. When you are done with your left leg, go back down and focus on your right fight. Repeat the visualization and focus on your other foot. From here, continue to go higher. From the pelvis, go higher to the abdomen, lower back, the navel, upper back, then the chest and shoulders.

Try to slow down in the areas where there are main organs, such as the lungs, heart, and stomach. Imagine your breath bringing healing energy to your organs. Now, bring your focus to your left fingers and hands then up toward your elbows and arms. Repeat the same technique until you've finished with both hands.

From here, bring your awareness to your neck, then up to your face. Give special attention to space right between your brows. Finally, finish by focusing on the top of your head. The last two areas can be especially receptive. You might end up feeling like you are floating and that your consciousness is more fluid in your own body.

When you are ready, pull your awareness away from your head, and bring your awareness back to your whole body. Feel your breath go in and out in waves.

After a few minutes, wriggle your toes and fingers and slowly open your hand. Return your awareness to normal and stretch a little before you get up.

Meditation With Visualizations

Visualizations can be added to your basic meditation techniques and can help develop a certain trait or attitude in you. When practicing certain visualization techniques, simply start with basic breathing meditation. When you feel at peace and still, you can start your visualization.

The Sanctuary

Visualizing a sanctuary or a refuge is a great place to recharge your energy and shake off some stress and anxiety. This technique can also help in healing certain mental and emotional wounds.

Do your standard, basic meditation until your mind is relatively still and your body relaxed (preferably for five minutes).

Start visualizing a place where you have always felt safe. It might be a real place from your past or just something you imagined. As long as it makes you feel safe and protected, then it should work. Be as specific as you want. If you imagine yourself in a garden, then what plants can be found there? Are there singing birds and trees that provide shade? Do your best to make the visualization as vivid as possible.

Once you have found your safe place, simply allow the sensation of peacefulness, safety, and comfort permeate across your entire being. Know that you are safe here and that no one can touch you here. Within your sanctuary, you can explore all your emotions, even those of hurt, fear, and humiliation.

Stay in your sanctuary for as long as you need, and make sure to end your session by reaffirming the positive emotions you feel in your safe place.

Best Meditation Techniques

Meditation is not rocket science, but that is not to say it is entirely easy either.

The following are three of the best meditation techniques that you may find very helpful. I urge you to read on.

Relaxation Response

This exercise is known to have benefits, like reducing stress levels as well as other positive effects that can be derived from relaxation. Practicing the Relaxation Response for 15-20 minutes a day will no doubt help to reduce your stress levels significantly.

Sit quietly in a place where you will not be disturbed.

The process may take a while, so for more effectiveness, make yourself comfortable for the entire process.

Walking Meditation

A walking meditation (which is the simplest form of moving meditation) can be practiced anywhere, at any time. Some people find it difficult to sit still, and some people suffer from anxiety attacks that worsen during meditation. If this is the case, walking meditation might be a more effective method of meditation compared to relaxation meditation.

The fact that it is termed "walking meditation" does not mean it is the same thing as simply taking a walk. It requires deliberate attention and concentration, which is what makes it different from a simple stroll.

You can't say you are practicing a walking meditation while you are at the same time making a phone call or listening to something on a tablet. It does not work that way!

You need to consciously put one foot in front of the other, align your focus on the universe, feel the ground beneath you as you take each step, and let the wind caress your skin—now that is walking meditation.

If you have a maze nearby, then count yourself lucky, because doing a maze-walk is an awesome way to perform walking meditation.

In as much the same way as when you are doing a relaxation meditation, you need to gently discard any unwanted thoughts that you may encounter as you walk.

Conclusion

Congratulations on finishing the book!

I'm passionate about meditation and have made every effort to help you understand how to meditate so that you too can experience the transformational benefits that it has to offer.

I hope this book gave you all the necessary information you needed to understand meditation better and apply it to your life in order to reduce stress and anxiety and achieve unending success.

www.ingramcontent.com/pod-product-compliance
Lightning Source LLC
Chambersburg PA
CBHW070708250726

48662CB00001B/316